AFRICAN IMAGES

AFRICAN IMAGES:

Recent Studies and Text in Cinema

Edited by

Maureen Eke

Kenneth W. Harrow

Emmanuel Yewah

Africa World Press, Inc.

P.O. Box 1892

Trenton, NJ 08607

P.O. Box 48

Asmara, ERITREA

Africa World Press, Inc.

P.O. Box 1892
Trenton, NJ 08607

P.O. Box 48
Asmara, ERITREA

Cover Design: Jonathan Gullery

Library of Congress Cataloging-in-Publication data

African images : Studies in cinema and texts / edited by Maureen N. Eke, Kenneth W. Harrow, Emmanuel Yewah.– 1st Africa World Press, Inc., ed.

       p. cm.– (Annual selected papers of the ALA, ISSN 1093-2976; no. 8)
    Selected papers, including interviews, of the Twenty-third Annual Conference of The African Literature Association which was a celebration of African cinema, in recognition of which it recieved the title "FESPACO Nights in Michigan," held Apr. 1997 in East Lansing Mich.
  Includes bibliographical references and index.
   ISBN 0-86543-819-6 (cloth) -- ISBN 0-86543-820-X (paper)
   1. Motion pictures--Africa--Congresses. 2. African literature--20th century--History and criticism--Congresses. I.Eke, Maureen N. II.Harrow, Kenneth W. III. Yewah, Emmanuel. IV. African Literature Association. Meeting (23rd: 1997: East Lansing, Mich.) V. Series

PN1993.5.A35 A372 2000
79. 43'75'096--dc21

                               99-059841

ANNUAL SELECTED PAPERS OF THE ALA

23rd Annual Meeting of the African Literature Association
FESPACO Nights in Michigan: African Film & Literature
held in East Lansing, Michigan from April 16 to 19, 1997
sponsored by Michigan State University

Series Editor: Hal Wylie

The ALA is an independent professional society founded in 1974. Membership is open to scholars, teachers and writers from every country. The ALA exists primarily to facilitate the attempts of a world-wide audience to appreciate the creative efforts of African writers and authors. The organization welcomes the participation of all who are interested and concerned with African literature. While we hope for a constructive interaction between scholars and artists, the ALA as an organization recognizes the primacy of African peoples in shaping the future of African literature.

The ALA publishes the quarterly *ALA Bulletin* for its members. Membership is for the calendar year and available on the following terms (U.S. funds): African students studying in Africa, $5; Income under $15,000, $15; Income from $15,000 to $35,000, $30; Income over $35,000, $40. ALA Headquarters: Contact Prof. Anne Adams, Director, Africana Studies and Research Center, Cornell University, 310 Triphammer Road, Ithaca, New York 14850-2599; Tel. 607-255-0415; Fax: 607-255-0784; e-mail: ava2@cornell.edu.

CONTENTS

Section 1

INTRODUCTION

1

Introduction

The twenty-third annual conference of the African Literature Association was a celebration of African cinema, in recognition of which it received the title, somewhat tongue-in-cheek, "FESPACO Nights in Michigan." As those who have attended the real FESPACO would know, the showings constitute a veritable festival in all senses of the word, and for the ALA conference this was also the case as there were many daily projections of films, as well as roundtables and special sessions devoted to Africa's many gifted filmmakers. Among those filmmakers who attended the conference were Salem Mekuria, Ngozi Onwurah, Tsitsi Dangarembga, Bassek ba Kobhio, Jean-Pierre Bekolo, François Woukoache, Djibril Diop Mambety, Assia Djebar, Gaston Kaboré, Ola Balogun, John Akomfrah. Manthia Diawara, appearing both as a filmmaker and as a film critic, was joined by Trinh T Minh-ha in a special session dealing with the anthropological gaze on Africa. The film critics Keyan Tomaselli, N. Frank Ukadike, and Phil Rosen, joined a distinguished list of scholars and cineastes, all of whom graced the conference with their images, words, and presence.

Although there were other distinguished panelists who merit mention, I will stop with the above list whose work bears particularly upon the theme of the conference, African cinema. As their presence indicated, African cinema has moved quickly in the past 40 years, since the independence of Ghana in 1957, or, from another perspective, in the 42 years since Paulin Vieyra and Mamadou Sarr's *Afrique sur Seine* was made in Paris in 1955. Whereas Sembène Ousmane is so often taken as the "father" of African cinema, what is often ignored in the appreciation of his considerable influence are those other strains of creativity that did not fall easily into the mold of "committed" work.

Djibril Diop Mambety's *Badou Boy* dates to 1970, and attests to the beginning of a remarkable career of filmmaking along the cusps of realism, surrealism, and allegory. Mambety's return to filmmaking with his monumental *Hyènes* (1992) and his no less inspired *Le Franc* (1995) represented high points in recent African cinema, just as his death in June of 1998 represented one of the great losses for the cinema. His early films opposed the dominant trends of mimetic realism and an engagé cinema committed to the amelioration of society. Now one can see in the works of a younger generation of filmmakers new attention to autobiographical self-inspection, once considered a form of bourgeois self-indulgence, or to symbolic, parodic, or carnivalesque representations, in which the binary model of education versus entertainment no longer suffices. No less serious in intent than the older styles, no less committed to values that are grounded in African soil, films such as Bekolo's *Aristotle's Plot* (1995) and Woukoache's *Asientos* (1995) attest to the younger generation's determination to find a mode of expression that is not moored to the past, and that dances its own dance, even when labeled by critics as post-colonial or post-modern.

Any study of the serious work of querying cinematic images of Africa, along with the male gaze or the eurocentric gaze on Africa, would have to begin with Trinh T. Minh-ha's *Reassemblage* (1982), and would now have to also include Manthia Diawara's *Rouch in Reverse* (1996), a work on the father of cinéma vérité, Jean Rouch. The term "reverse" includes, in one sense, the notion of looking back, looking from the perspective of those once taken as the object of the documentary filmmaker's or anthropologist's gaze—that is, in one scenario, the woman, in another the African, and in a third, the African woman. But the reversal of the gaze also entails a turn towards the political realm, and is now conveyed in those splendid portraits of self, those introspective works about family and society, that have been generated in recent years by such filmmakers as David Achkar (*Allah Tantou*-1990) and Raoul Peck (*Lumumba*-1992). Equally effective in taking film along that axis of exploration has been Salem Mekuria, whose *Deluge* (1996) takes us back to the chaotic and painful years of the revolution in Ethiopia in the late 1960s, seen from the perspective of the present, and along the line of vision of Mekuria's daughter. Indeed, many of the most successful works in the past decade have been forms of testimonial cinema that explore the past in ways that have been either neglected or repressed.

Most prominent among those explorers, both in literature and film, has been Assia Djebar, perhaps the most eloquent and creative voice raised in anguished response to the ways in which women have been abused, both in the past during the colonial period, and in the present struggle experienced in Algeria. The voice of that struggle has been heard in her well-known fiction, but is also brilliantly captured in her films, *La Zerda ou Les Chants de l'oubli* (1980) and *La Nouba des femmes du mont Chenoua* (1978). In recognition of her exceptional courage and inspiring words, she was awarded the African Literature Association's Fonlon-Nichols prize for 1997, and her eloquent speech at the occasion of that award is reproduced in this volume.

The continued growth of African cinema has been guaranteed in part by the work of such major, well-known cineastes as Ola Balogun and Gaston Kaboré, who have been faithful to the task of giving their societies knowledge of themselves in a positive light. They have inspired new generations for whom the struggle against such ills of yesterday as slavery, or the unfortunate heritage of a colonial past, has remained relevant, as well as for those still concerned with the ongoing need to capture the experience of Africa's traditions, as in Onwurah's *Monday's Girls* (1993), a film on initiation rites of Ijaw girls. Ba Kobhio's *Sango Malo* (1991), a portrait of a Cameroonian village caught in the struggle between the generations to reform their system of education, follows along these lines, while Akomfrah has established himself as one of the foremost chroniclers of the Diasporan experience. In *Last Angel of History* (1995), he has created a hyper-modern portrait of an unusual side of the Black experience, that dealing with science fiction, and futurist avant-garde music and culture.

Like Djebar, and indeed Sembène, whose names were first established as authors, Dangarembga has also branched into filmmaking so as to reach a wider audience. Her film *Everyone's Child* (1997) uses image as well as word to bring to the audience the dramatic situation created by AIDS, especially for Africa's orphaned children.

The present volume contains a number of texts that relate to the above body of films, including interviews with Onwurah, Bekolo, and Kaboré, Djebar's Fonlon-Nichols speech, and the text of Bekolo's *Aristotle's Plot*. In addition, scholarly essays on African cinema, focusing upon particular aspects of national cinemas or on individual films, give the volume a unique place in the literature of film criticism.

S. Ekema Agbaw examines Cameroonian cinema, with particular attention placed upon three recent films whose filmmakers are currently creating a renaissance in Cameroonian filmmaking. Bassek Ba Khobio's *Sango Malo* (1991) has stirred considerable interest because of the successful employment of social realism in raising key questions about retrograde social power in Cameroon's rural educational system. Jean-Pierre Bekolo's *Quartier Mozart* (1992) strikes out in a new, brilliant direction in the comedic portrayal of gender politics in the popular quartier of Yaounde. And in *Afrique, je te plumerai*, Jean-Marie Teno has continued the tradition of engaged Cameroonian cinematography that goes back to the work of Dikongue-Pipa and Daniel Kamwa in the 1970s, although his docu-fictional technique bears all the ironic reflexivity of post-modernism. Together these three filmmakers, along with other Cameroonians such as François Woukoache, have succeeded in producing a significant corpus of films whose role in Cameroonian society is linked to the social revolution of the 1990s. It is that context that Agbaw links to social and political change in his explication of the films.

Specialized studies on individual films, including essays by Touria Khannous on Djebar's *La Nouba des femmes du mont Chenoua*; by Jarrod Hayes on Nouri Bouzid's *Homme de cendres* (1986); and by Stephen Zacks on *La Haine* (1995). Khannous turns her attention to the little studied issue of the "cultural reality and history of the Algerian woman in French cinematic discourse." It is the discourse dealing with the Algerian revolution that Djebar has revisited in her two films, *La Zerda* and especially for our interest, *La Nouba*. Perhaps no writer today has done as much as Djebar in highlighting that forgotten and repressed role of the Algerian woman in revolutionary and post-revolutionary Algerian society. Khannou draws upon subaltern studies, and responds to Spivak's question, "can the subaltern speak?", adding Djebar's questions, "can she gaze," can she be an agent in history. *La Nouba* is Djebar's response to these fundamental feminist issues.

Hayes explores another closed, forbidden, silenced space, that of gay politics in Tunisian society, as represented in Nouri Bouzid's *Man of Ashes* (1986). For Haynes, it is the play initiated by a literal writing of the past as it impinges upon the film's protagonist that points to the larger allegorical implications of the film. Individual gay politics inscribe Tunisia's collective history on society in the passage from colonial to independent state, a passage in which the marks left by past violations and rapes become visible in the present lives of the young men. Positing colonialism as historical rape, Hayes is thus positioned to explore the conflict between Jameson's broadbrush thesis describing Third World literature as necessarily national allegories and Aijaz Ahmad's critique of Jameson.

Stephen Zacks also concerns himself with the cultural context within which one of the most effective "banlieu" films has been placed: that of the world of Parisian suburban (i.e., "ghetto") youth, which serves as the backdrop for Mathieu Kassovitz's *La Haine*. Zacks recreates for us the ambiance and the argot (*verlan*) in which not only the syllables are *inverted*, but the socially dominant values as well. The theoretical issues bearing upon Zacks's own personal experience and its relationship to sociological criticism are heightened in a film that is self-consciously social realist, and that raises social issues in an intensely personal fashion. Film as construct; film as product or reflection of experience—these are the twin poles whose oppositionality is explored in this chapter. The resonance of these issues for the larger corpus of African cinema as a vehicle for social change remains important as long as the pedagogic function continues in films such as *Sango Malo* or *Afrique, je te plumerai.*

Finally, the African Literature Association still remains faithful to its primary charge of the study and support of African literature, for which issues of representation, staging, image, and narrative remain no less central than they do for cinema. The present volume also includes four chapters on various aspects of literature. Linda Helstern's study of Brathwaite's *Middle Passages* (1992) is, appropriately, devoted to Brathwaite's innovative, brilliant use of what he terms *Sycorax Video Style.* Helstern explicates the arcane references Brathwaite employs in the poetry of *Middle Passages,* and in particular examines the glyphs, the iconography, the extraordinary visual imagery Brathwaite created with his computer so as to elevate the visual experience of the poems beyond the immediacy of their condition as verbal signifiers. The Mesoamerican calendar, in all its brilliance, forms a complex and intriguing centerpiece to the volume—a sign for the re- encoding of New World history Brathwaite attempts through this volume.

In another twist on the cinematic dimension of African literature, Lydie Moudileno examines the role of the cinematic systems of delivery as conduits for the colonial imaginary in Sylvain Bemba's *Rêves portatifs* (1979). Bemba recreates the world of preindependence Africa in which colonial authorities gave their approval to the taste machines formed by American westerns, Indian melodramas, and French comedies. Acculturation was a preeminent colonial goal, and the delivery of a selected corpus of films played an important role in the ideological apparatus of the colonial state. Moudelino draws upon Roger Caillois's *Les Jeux et les hommes* (1958) so as to examine the movie theatre as a "playing field," a space in which a complex range of playing activities can be analyzed—activities in which the intrusion of the real, as in Zacks's consideration of *La Haine,* is shaped by the "contamination" between the separate universes of fiction and "reality."

Carmela Garritano's explores another wide-eyed "stage," that occasioned by the oral tales of the Beautiful Daughter (perhaps best known in the version given in Amos Tutuola's *Palm-wine Drinkard* [1954]). If not allegorical, the tale is at least quintessentially West African, as it reappears in different versions by Ogali Ogali, Ama Ata Aidoo, and finally, in a folktale published in a collection edited by Roger Abrahams. Following Chandra Mohanty's definitions of Third World feminism, Garritano traces the ways in which this tale is deployed through various patriarchal strategies so as to conceal "heterogeneity and ambiguity." In contrast to the naturalizing ideologies embraced by various performers of the tale, Garritano's reading follows lines suggested by Bhabha, shifting away from humanist paradigms that lead to normalization and institutionalization of dominant values. Here it is the analysis not of allegory but of stereotypical discourse that provides for the possibilities of resistance to patriarchy, and for an opening to the productive ambiguities in the different versions of the tale—ambiguities that inform Bhabha's embrace of the concept of hybridity. Interestingly, Garritano contrasts Aidoo's successful deployment of the disruptive voice of female desire with the normalizing tendencies in the three "male" versions of the tale.

Lastly, in another look at the transformation of a common tale into two literary works, Lamia Ben Youssef's examines the image of the black slave in two north African folktales, Marguerite Taos Amrouche's "Le Grain Magique" and Abdelaziz Aroui's "The Black Merchant." In these two versions of the faithful wife or sister, a Black figure—a merchant or a slave—outwits an Arab dupe, a husband or brother, who must be rescued by a faithful female. Following Ben Youssef's Proppian analysis, it is the clash between an older matriarchal order and the more recent Islamic patriarchy that underlies the different versions of the tale. The defenses of an orthodox Muslim patriarchy take the form of folk wisdom in which the social order is naturalized. Underlying the defenses can be traced the apprehension over the power of female sexuality to disrupt the Muslim social order. In both cases, it is the figure of an old woman, Settoute, a recurrent figure in North African folklore, who is demonized, and who is here reread through the optic provided by Kristeva's *Powers of Horror*. Finally, the alliance between black and female figures gives particular significance to this conventional characterization: it is the black woman's ascendancy in each case that conveys the threat to the forces of order.

From cinematic image to folktale imagery, icons of resistance and identity, essentialized, problematized, ambiguous, and then naturalized, continue to recur. As Garritano reminds us in her study of the Tutuola version of the familiar tale, his work, like much of African literature and cinema, lies "in the interstices of West African [or North African] and European discourses and, like a palimpsest, holds layers of meaning which despite erasure, leave imprints." Now we may say we are on the trail of such traces as they appear in their visual forms, as with past trackings of the all-sacrosanct Word. Each of the essays contained in this volume, in its own way is inspired by those imprints, indelibly marked on each frame that is projected into the dark, as well as on each page that we read.

—Kenneth W. Harrow

NOTE

The following texts represent major critical studies of African cinema:

Bakari, Imruh and Mbye Cham, eds. *African Experiences of Cinema*. London: British Film Institute, 1996.

Diawara, Manthia. *African Cinema*. Bloomington: Indiana U P, 1992.

Harrow, Kenneth, ed. *African Cinema: Postcolonial and Feminist Readings*. Lawrenceville, NJ: Africa World Press, 1999.

______ ed. *African Cinema*. Fall 1995, 26.3, (special issue on African cinema).

______ ed. *African Cinema*, a special issue of *African Cinema*, no. 19, 1997, (on the topic of women and African cinema).

Martin, Michael T., ed. *Cinemas of the Black Diaspora*. Detroit: Wayne State U P, 1995.

Ukadike, N. Frank. *Black African Cinema*. Berkeley: University of California P, 1994.

Section 2

FILMMAKERS' WORDS

2

ACCEPTANCE SPEECH[1]
Fonlon-Nichols Prize

by Assia Djebar

Michigan State University
April 1997.

1

I will make so bold as to say, right from the beginning, how heavy it feels, this Fonlon-Nichols Prize that you are giving me; how heavy it feels to carry. For, out of the four African writer-laureates who have preceded me, two have departed much too soon. We know it all too well: one, Ken Saro-Wiwa, the victim—so much so—of state-sanctioned military oppression (one of the seven scourges of modern Africa); the other, Sony Labou-Tansi, so swiftly carried away by the new disease that has no remedy, especially in Africa.

Two writers, whose words, so rich and so particularly original, have remained suspended: they are here, present among us today (many of their personal friends are here with us, in this auditorium, I am sure). They tell us, as much with their corpus that has become their own unerasable shadow, as with their martyrdom and their death; they remind us, those of us who are survivors from this continent more than ever dispossessed, that *the words we speak and the words we write must henceforth make their way between the hangman's noose and the mortuary.*

What future, then, offers itself to a writer, who, far away in the multiple "hot spots" of Africa—whether Ethiopia or Sudan, yesterday; Rwanda, Nigeria or Liberia, next; now Zaire . . . and over the past five years, already, Algeria—what future to a writer who, having refused exile or being now unable to avail oneself of the possibility of exile, may end up loving one's homeland more than one's pen, choosing one's homeland over one's art? Yes, indeed, will our (brother and sister) writers, those already well-known and who have become thereby more easy targets; or those less known, whose very obscurity now protects them but keeps them silent too, will they be able once more to recapture within the narrowing path the live movement of their own singular intellectual life/practice, of their own writer's thoughts?

As for the two prior laureates whom I evoked, they faced, one, strangulation in spite of world protests, and, the other, the insidious, incurable poison.

And that is why this fifth Fonlon-Nichols Prize is, as I mentioned earlier, so heavy to bear; under its symbolic weight, am I not going to weaken, to stumble, eventually, to fall silent? Because of my emotion, of course, our own collective emotion here; but I would venture as well, I dare here a French neologism—because of "inconsolation."

For, how am I now to write and keep "this raw unforgetting alive?" Indeed, our two brother-writers, Ken and Sony, are not the only ones. They merely lead the long procession of an immense crowd of anonymous ones—women and children included—especially these past two years, those whose photographed faces scream under our fingers as we open the folded newspapers to the page devoted to African news.

Ken and Sony are with us today . . . And with them, behind them, around them, [stands] Africa, her countries that should have been the richest, the most creative, an Africa who screams her silence. At times, I feel, [she screams] while the world looks away indifferently, and here we are, survivors scattered here and there by this indifference, this turning it all into something banal that makes insomniacs of us all.

2

So, how is one to write? To write as I do, quickly, hastily, in order to bear feverish witness to the fear of a possible suppression . . . might convulsions be fitting only for exodus and civil wars? To write an African fiction, to unfold a story with hurried, yet passionate faithfulness, how is one to attain truth that is serene (therefore, from a distance) in the midst of this chaos situated way up from the battle (and, therefore, riding the void of utopia)?

In a word, how to remain a writer whose thinking is, perforce, accidental (serendipitous)—but a thinking that can still fly; which is to say, that can resist—and this in spite of being battered with the ever increasing sorrows to which we must bear witness. To go on creating, in my case, novels, films, poems, might it not be but the bitter manifestation—albeit it one that is still alive—of our powerlessness?

Such are the questions with which I wrestle each day of my new American exile, questions that haunt undoubtedly any writer from Africa or the Third World, wherever s/he happens to land in order to write, maddened back to savage wildness and apparent chaos.

3

I will end this speech with wondering aloud whether, when you chose me as the fifth Fonlon-Nichols laureate, you did not mean to honor as much the woman from Africa, novelist, and film maker, as simply, the woman from Algeria?

In one of the short stories I published this past month of March 1997 (Publisud)—stories, alas, that most often are but my own reading of, my own listening to, from Paris or the United States, this Algerian tragedy that, thirty years later, has again started its uncontrollable mechanism..

In one of these "short stories" (English in the original), a young woman school teacher in Algiers, retells, with commentaries a story from to her students; it is the one called "The Dismembered Woman," a martyrdom invented by Sheherazade.

But, in what passes for reality in Algeria today, the teacher who speaks in the shadow of the Sultana, ends up beheaded before her own students. Several such murders of women, school teachers, and professors *have* taken place in this very manner these past few months.

In my own short story, the beheaded Algerian woman, her blood-oozing head sitting on the desk to face the children, continues to speak her tale. She knows the ending by heart, the moment when the Sultan forgives his own wife (woman) and all women, and, therefore, (forgives) her, the story-teller who speaks it in blood and mutilation after the murderers have departed.

Therefore, please forgive me for concluding now as a simple Algerian woman and humble storyteller; the funeral phantasmagoric sometimes becomes our only possible response to a violence whose very meaning escapes us.

It is, in truth, the *why?* of a violence such as this, one that tattoos every single day the whole body of Africa; as for me, it is this *why?* that gyrates us all into a fatal vertigo that I am attempting to grasp in my stories.

We are the ones, writers and intellectuals from Africa, to whom media from elsewhere turn for a commentary on each and every one of our home countries [stuck] within a gaping fissure, a disaster. For me, as far as Algeria is concerned and throughout the past five years of this tragedy that will not end, I have refused "the commentary;" it would be too convenient, and the request comes most often for the benefit of a public, excuse the phrase, sometimes satiated, a public of satiated voyeurs.

I ask myself most often, because of my own simple suffering, a woman's suffering, *"how is one to keep Algeria quiet?"* To keep her quiet, the better to carry her, to take her with me wherever I go, to cradle within me her throbbing, grieving sorrow . . . to carry her, just like the Algerian woman of the story, a severed head, who persists in speaking . . .

CONCLUSION

I was wondering to myself in the plane today what force there might exist that best could unite us and help us identify with each other—us, people who have come from the four corners of Africa. Could it be Death, a death that speaks to us, a hallucination that opens the dialogue and demands a response?

If we can no longer avoid our dead, those too recently departed— those whose work remains unfinished and whose young lives have been severed— at least let us gather around them, but in an *authentically African manner*. I have a model in mind, what is called "le grand retournement" (the great turning over) according to the ancestral ritual of the Madagascar Merinas.

Yes, I would certainly adopt this ritual: take out from their graves our absent ones, our bruised ones, our martyred ones; turn over their bones in public and in the open air; change their shrouds. And all through this, just like the ancient Merinas of yore, I would *sing*; I would speak (to them) *in joyful* tones; I would make of it a festival and a celebration. In short, I would turn Death, she who has become inseparable from us, into a ceremonial of beauty, of inventive verb, of life.

I did say in the beginning, did I not, that Africa and its thousands and thousands of victims screamed, screamed in vain to others? And, so, let us all not forget, we who are together here today, that Africa also writes herself in music, in all literature that is defiant.

Thank you, therefore, both for giving me this Prize and for lending me your ears.

NOTE

Translated from French by Clarisse Zimra, Dept. of English, Southern Illinois University, Carbondale, Illinois.

3

ARISTOTLE'S PLOT

by Jean Pierre Bekolo

[Text from Jean Pierre Bekolo's *ARISTOTLE'S PLOT*, a film made for the celebration of the hundred years of cinema, followed by his comments on the film.]

E.T. is an African filmmaker who returns home to Zimbabwe to show his films. He finds the movie theaters filled with gangster types who have adopted the roles of Western characters from popular Hollywood or kung fu films of violence, like those of Arnold Schwartznegger. The leader of the gangsters is called Cinema The voiceover by the narrator is what follows.

1

I was in my bush of Africa chewing kola nut with my grandfather when I heard the drums telling me that I had a phone call from London. The British Film Institute wanted me to make a film to celebrate the centenary of cinema. I asked them who else was in the list. Martin Scorsese, Stephen Frears, Jean-Luc Godard . . . . Then I started wondering why me? Is it Christian charity or political correctness? It was like accepting the challenge of someone who is already standing on the finish line without agreeing first on the starting line.

Before I leave, my grandfather explains to me that a long time back we knew that thing they call cinema in Africa. I decide to celebrate the centenary of cinema only if my film is the best.

2

I started my research with Aristotle's *Poetics*, the bedrock of European storytelling. I wanted to beat these guys at their own game. I needed a good story. The arena will be contemporary Africa. The protagonist is the filmmaker who inspired me the most, Essomba Tourneur. E.T as we used to call him had that something special; he desperately desired to such a degree that it became an issue of life or death. Essomba Tourneur was put in jail after he returned from France where he graduated with famous French directors. His wife committed suicide and his children went with his wife's parents who never accepted that their daughter married a suffering artist. ET refused to be a puppet. He was an *artiste maudit*. Shem's malediction weighed heavy on him, and he bore on his shoulders the weight of original sin. But ET, who thought he was an angel, had to admit he was a spirit. And an African spirit. Because otherwise, how else explain the effort the Gods had made in his regard?

The truth is Essomba Tourneur was worrying them. Since his arrival home, Essomba was tailed by the police. For the government, a cineaste was more or less the same thing as a gangster. Because the best school for becoming a thug remained the cinema. The only thing they gave back to him were his films. E.T's antagonists were faceless; the police and the gangsters were part of them. My grandfather once told me when I decided I wouldn't be a doctor, "A filmmaker is a criminal who.doesn't have enough personality to become a gangster."

4

According to Aristotle's *Poetics*, my story had to inspire fear and pity. ET was choosing his enemy to match his own strengh. Even the governement was not threatening him. The rascals who provoked him without knowing whom they were dealing with, would have to learn about the man they had foolishly defied.

5

E.T's antagonists were faceless. That's why they had chosen the silliest cop to handle Essomba's case, and the government had never tried to view our greatest director's films. Essomba was a subversive and they had decided to crush him Hollywood style; thus: "They put pressure on you, you change alone."

6

Because of their loss of memory and their roles as film characters, the gang was an obstacle to Essomba Tourneur's goal. Their whole life entailed hanging out in front of the theater and watching films; that's how they ended up finding their imaginary film personas. It was only a matter of time before the personas would replace the real beings, the ones they had once thought were themselves.

7

Essomba was really too good for them. He no longer understood his country, the one to which he had wanted to return. The rules had changed. Invented stories had taken the place of reality.

8

Essomba was a brain. He was what the country needed to shake it up in order to become a world power. He played with the contradictions of the system to achieve his goals. The governement won a few points by coopting Essomba. No more gangster university. That was the only positive thing, because Essomba attracted the wrong audience. His fellows were identifying more with an Eastwood than a Kocumbo lost in his native bush in conflict with spirits. If you wanted to tell someone about spirits, you might consider making a film about Thomas Sankara who said one day, "Kill Sankara, you will have 20 Sankaras." A film that would end up in the ditch [???] because of no funding.

9

My story was now on track. As I was following Aristotle's principles, I wondered why Chapter Two of *Poetics* was missing. Then I went to do more research. As I went deeper, I had more and more questions. Why had the second chapter of Aristotle's *Poetics* disappeared? Why is the Sphinx's nose locked in the British Museum? Why did Oakley strongly oppose [????] Dawson? Why do they prefer the Cro-Magnon man to his collegue of Grimaldi? Why are we still talking about Thales or Pythagoras? Why did Bokassa proclaim himself emperor like Napoleon? Why are African filmmakers always asked political questions? Where is the Black Man today? As if they all have to be Nelson Mandelas. Can Nelson Mandela make a film? Why is an African filmmaker always a young, upcoming, promising filmmaker until he reaches 80 years old, and then he becomes the ancestor,the father, the wise man?

10

African cinema couldn't answer these questions. It was nothing more than folklore. Bruce Willis on a mission to the colonies. How could I have explained this to that stupid cop who kept harassing me with surrealist questions?

11

My characters went out of my control. Armed with their degrees, the unemployed gangsters hurried to get a job: men of action [???]. They would take a vow a to the cult to action. The catharsis. What my grandfather calls the bitterness and the sweetness of life. The violence necessary to the salvation of humanity. Inspire fear and pity, that is the mission. Without fear and pity, no redemption. Inch Allah, Amen . . . .

12

These young cultural bastards, like those now found all over the world, thought they were stealing the heart of Hollywood while they were ignoring the fact that they were going back to their roots. Nature never made the same thing twice. If you were made white, there was little chance that you would be made black one day; too bad. Cinema wasn't born twice. It was in Africa twenty-three centuries ago.

13

I don't know if it's the blood that changed Essomba who couldn't help undergoing transformations. A vane couldn't have done a better job. He was showing me that a jacket can have more than two sides.

14

Even the brother who came to Africa to know where he came from was out of my control. He'd have a clearer idea of where he was going now.

15

Because a plot is made of a series of events that have a beginning, I started suspecting that my invitation to be part of the British Film Institute celebration of 100 years of cinema could only be a plot twenty-three centuries old. Aristotle's plot. Even if I was trying to avoid it, I was already trapped in the formula, the "how to." Today, Aristotle's formula produces gangsters, magicians, corrupt governments, suffering artists, forgers ... . But all that is not very dangerous because the sweetness of the kola nut comes after the bitterness.

I was now sure that if our world inspires fear and pity, it's not by accident. Aristotle, like an alchemist, thought that by mixing fear and pity in a story, it would produce a catharsis that would save the human race from violence. My grandfather's theory of kola nut.

I picked up the Bible to find a way out. Even there, I was already condemned for original sin. In addition to that, God put a curse on the Black man. The same God who is spreading suffering and pain with the false hope that one day everything would be all right. A God who condemned me to be a filmmaker working in a bar to make a living, hoping that the bitterness of the kola nut would turn sweet. A God who knows that the day I would make my film, not the British Film Institute's, he would be unmasked. Sometimes I think about this and I have a lot of respect for the guy who invented candy.

And Cinema and his friends agreed with me.

16

Then what my grandfather told me began to run through my mind. What is an initiation ceremony? People in pursuit of a goal, whose actions form scenes divided into crisis, confrontation, climax and resolution. All wrapped up with pictures and sound. Stories, images, sounds, narrations, rhythms. Is there anything here that is not African? Fantastic and mystic? Walt Disney, we got; Lion King, we got; sex, action, violence, we got; massacres, we got; comedians, music, we got; Paul Simon, we got; dance and dancers, we got; beauty, ugliness, we got; thinkers, we got; Aristotle, catharsis, kola nuts, we got; to make it short, what don't we have?

We don't want our cinema to come from life. Because when it comes from life, it is dead. It's like a difficult childbirth: the mother or the baby? Life or cinema? Because when cinema starts happening in the real world [???], you are dead, it is dead, we are all dead.

17

Now, the life of aspiring gangsters became an imitation of ignoble actions thought to cause fear and pain [???], in a colorful language, full of references. In short, a tragedy. Except that instead of imitating life, they were imitating an imitation of life.

18

This is why Cinema went round and round for two days, ignoring that his pathetic wheelings wouldn't change any of the eternal essence of things. That's why Essomba Tourneur came to fulfill their expectations.

19

As my grandfather used to say, "Death has never killed nobody."

I decided then to stop following Aristotle's principles, to bring the dead back to life and change the rules of the game.

20

The cop arrested Essomba and Cinema, leaving in a police van.

21

New shot, initial scene: commentary on the opening of the dialogue.

How many times have you heard a story of a cop and gangsters? How many times have you heard a story of a filmmaker? You have already seen this railway crossing. I call it now *the railway crossing of the three deads,* a tribute to all the dead victims of Aristotle's plot. In his time, the happy ending was necessary. Aristotle's disciples understood that the rules they thought were immutable would be changing soon. Death did not exist anymore and the idea of ending a story had to be reinvented.

22

Where did the cameraman go? He has run in front of the scene. He didn't understand himself that it was cinema. But could we blame him? In this world where the dead and the living are linked, how could we distinguish the real from the fake, fable from reality? Come on, don't worry. You are not the only one who didn't get it all.

Comment

Comment on *Aristotle's Plot* by Jean-Pierre Bekolo, Recorded in Boston, November 1997

I was invited by the British Film Institute to contribute to the commemoration of one hundred years of cinema along with other directors: Martin Scorsese, Bertollucci, Godard. That's why I decided to make *Aristotle's Plot,* a film that would reflect the theme of the project. It tells the story of three broad characters: a cop who has been asked by his boss to find out why people can die in one film and reappear in another; a very bitter filmmaker who, having studied abroad, has come back home with high expectations just to find himself suddenly homeless; the gang made up of the leader called Cinema because he has watched over ten thousand films and other gang members: Schwartznegger, Vandam, Sadam, Cobra, Nikita, Essomba Tourneur (ET).

Action begins when the filmmaker is kicked out of the theater by the gang. Once out, he alerts the police who, in turn kick the gang out of the theater. Outside, the gang experiences the beauty of the landscape, the countryside and decides to steal some of the films in order to open their own cinema in the village. What they do not know, however, is that the filmmaker has gone back to the theater to show African films. The only person watching the film is an African-American searching for his roots. Realizing that his films have been stolen, the filmmaker acts swiftly and decisively killing all the gang members in the process. And as my grandfather used to say, death never kills anybody. I tried to make an action-packed film in the best tradition of Hollywood and at the same time according to Aristotle's formula. And that explains the two dimensions of the film: killing everybody and bringing them back to life.

I decided not to make documentaries for the simple reason that, in the case of Africa, they tend to focus more on reality, indeed ethnology, while ignoring the imaginative process. I have always been fascinated by the power of the imagination and its capacity to dream up a world. I believe strongly that imagination is the driving force behind Western cultures. Documentaries simply reduce that imagination to reality especially since for the West, Africa is already an imaginary space as reflected in such films as *Out of Africa* and many others. For *Aristotle's Plot* I couldn't use anything else but fiction in which I have put a lot of voiceover, that is, I have given voice to the I, a technique unfortunately missing in African cinema. I was once told that no one ever hears what Africans say or what they think. And by extension such a statement would seeem to suggest that Africans don't think at all.

It is true that there are specialists on Africa all over the world serving as its mouthpiece, but hardly do we hear individual African voices themselves. I am very individualistic, indeed I do exist. I think it's very important that people in Africa exist as individuals and not always through the community or the group. The film attempts to tell my own story; to convey my own perception of cinema, express my point of view, and define my own vision. One would certainly have a different point of view if another filmmaker had been asked to make the film. All the technical elements used—the film was shot on panvision, 35mm, ratio 1:185; the sound, dolby stereo like ultrastereo, which is like dolbystereo SR, makes it suitable for big screen showings.

When we talk about cinema, we should go back to some basic techniques of filmmaking. The debate has never been about film itself, but rather about money, politics or economics. Critics of African cinema contend that sometimes Western critics feel guilty to criticize and that they tend to be very complacent. On the other side, there are some who argue that Africa is so backward that there are no cinematic productions coming out of there to warrant any critical attention. Western critics point to the reluctance of people in Africa to critically evaluate African cinema on the grounds that its hard enough, given the various contexts, for Africans to make films and, therefore, feel that any effort should be strongly encouraged. Personally, I think such uncritical views will encourage mediocrity rather than inspire African filmmakers to produce quality films. Take for instance the Ouagadougou Film Festival; prior to this year (1997) when for the first time films were preselected, any African who made a feature length film was allowed to enter the competition. Therefore, one of the objectives of *Aristotle's Plot* is to reopen the debate on criticism of the African film industry.

It is interesting how people focus on technology and the techniques of filmmaking while ignoring the very important aspect of storytelling. I was a member of jury at the Montreal Film Festival in August and watched so many films that at the end I forgot most of them. What I still remember vividly is people's dramas all over the world, people struggling for survival. When the camera stops shooting, what remains is storytelling. To make films, one has to read books about how to write a sceenplay. Here one learns to create a story with a beginning, middle, and end as outlined in *Aristotle's Poetics*. I should point out that Aristotle's technique and that used in African storytelling do share one element, that is, tragedy. Besides that, however, and given my African background, I tend to see more drama, comedy, satire, and humor.

Aristotle's Plot is deliberately provocative as a strategy to generate debate. It questions established rules and attempts to develop some thoughts about the idea of plot which, in French, has the double meaning of intrigue and enplotment. An African filmmaker or storyteller must be innovative in his/her approach to filmmaking rather than simply borrow or, in fact, copy Western concepts read in books on how to write a screenplay. Even Ousmane Sembène whom I admire very much seems to have fallen prey to the Western storytelling mode. The question of influence is an important one and, God knows, I'm not immune to it as evidenced by my use of Aristotle's formula or my inclination for Hollywood. Sometimes I don't seem to be myself; I seem to lose control because my whole project is structured by someone else's formulation. Such ambivalence generates the type of engaging debate that I'm advocating here for the African cinema.

Looking back at my invitation to contribute to the series commemorating one hundred years of cinema when the independence of most African countries is barely three and one half decades, one cannot help but read in this apparently inclusive gesture a geopolitical game at play. A game in which, as the only African, I have become a pawn. Let me mention here that the production of the film was stopped for two years; this in part because the sponsors did little to mask their paternalistic attitude towards the only African in the series.

By creating a character named Cinema, I was trying to highlight those who goes to the movies, what films they watch, how those things fit together. The type of character I'm portraying is very relevant in that it tells us the kind of film they have been watching. What films do African people actually watch? The biggest gangs meet around movie theaters. And it is here that violence seen in the movies is acted out in their hangout near the theater. For instance, about 90% of the people around the cinema Rex in Douala are young people. I tried to capture their voices individually rather than as a collectivity.

Conceived in France, the film was shot with a French crew and edited by a French woman. The relationship between francophone African cinema and France, as in all other forms of relationship, has always been colored by suspicion which, in this case, has an influence on the choice of subject, content, and aesthetics. A film such as *Yaaba* for example shows clearly the French approach to filmmaking, especially as it relates to Africa. Everything seems minimal. Set in the country where people speak their language; there is no attempt to explore techniques of filmmaking: no costuming; a predominance of the naturalistic; a slow-pace; and, in many cases, a style reduced to ethnology. Moreover, there is a general lack of aesthetics which is, indeed, significan't in that it reinforces the false perception that Africa lacks any aesthetic appreciation or that there are more pressing concerns than the search for the Idea of beauty. And francophone African filmmaking seems to be a product of that way of thinking.

There is an interesting scene in *Yaaba* where two kids and a madman are burying an old lady; where in Africa would you have that? Even though set in Africa, that particular scene raises the question of whether the film was made by an African.

I'm more interested in the absurd. My first film *Quartier Mozart*, set in a popular quartier of Douala, sets the stage for exploring the idea of the absurd. What does Mozart have to do with that? Can anyone make the connection between Mozart and that quartier? I don't know it myself. The fact remains that colonialist adventurism in Africa highlighted the very notion of absurdity; of contradictions. I sometimes ask myself why I'm called Jean-Pierre, why I'm stuck with this name that I can't change because it defines my identity; everybody already knows me by that name. The opening song of *Aristotle's Plot* was made by a Cameroonian musician who calls himself Danny Hollywood. How absurd! That is precisely what I'm interested in showing; the absurd not so much as something negative but rather as the disparity between what one thinks one sees or hears, and what one really sees or hears. I don't like to make straightforward statements. I want to create doubt in people's minds and leave them thinking that they have found the truth.

Cinema is both character and the film itself. It has many levels and designs. At one level, Cinema is putting on a mask representing a movie theater at the beginning of a showing when the lights have just been turned off. From this mask comes the projection of the film. However, when the projectionist is killed, the screen becomes dark. While on one side of the mask the film is being projected onto the screen, on the other side people who are not in the film are trying to imitate the life in the film. So I do play with the lighting and visual images. I'm using the same aesthetic elements to make comments or to keep telling the story about film. Cobra's statement that this place is prehistoric Jurassic Park, shows that even in their own place the point of reference is becoming Western since the only way to describe the countryside when they see it for the first time is "prehistoric." It means that they have lost their own points of reference, their own culture, and the only thing they have left is a Western point of reference. It's true that there are many different ways of talking about the same thing. And I wouldn't say it's just about African cinema, but about things in general even though I had to focus on the African dimension.

Main characters are always heroes. Since in *Aristotle's Plot* characters are living under a dictatorship having someone like Sadam or Sankara called Schwarznegger and then identify with those who rise up and challenge the system, does indeed qualify them as heroes. What Hollywood films do is offer cathartic outlets for those victimized characters. Many of these characters, educated in the Hollywood tradition, are very much into politics, and when demonstrations are called, they are the first to take to the streets. Even though Hollywood films do not preach revolution, they do, however, construct heroes that the characters in this film seek to emulate.

The world I'm describing is certainly not a woman's world. Female characters appear occasionally to add diversity to the gang. Nikita is a strong woman on a par with strong men like Cobra, Cinema, Vandame, Schwarznegger. Nonetheless, her relationship with Cinema creates a conflict with other gang members, thereby revealing their outlaw status.

4

GASTON KABORE
INTERVIEWED

by Debra Boyd

DB: We're in the Kellogg Center at Michigan State University with Gaston Kaboré, Burkinabé film-maker and the 1997 winner of the Etalon de Yennenga (Stallion of Yennenga) prize for his film "Budd Yam," awarded during the 15th edition of FESPACO, the Pan-African Film and Television Festival of Ouagadougou, held every two years in Ouagadougou, Burkina Faso.

Gaston, thank you very much. To begin, would you speak a little about your background? Did you study film? What series of events led you to start making films?

GK: Thank you. Before undertaking film studies I studied history. I was at the Sorbonne in Paris where I completed the *licence*, the *maitrise*, and two certificates for concentrated studies in history that comprise the first year of preparation for the "doctorat de 3e" cycle which is a two year program. It seems that what first led me to cinema was my Masters degree in history, for which I had chosen, as a topic, "the image of black Africa in the illustrated press at the end of the 19th century." The point of departure for my discussion was the Berlin Conference of 1885, which authorized the balkanization of Africa in 1900, the end of the 19th century, and the beginning of the 20th century. I wanted to show in this work of historical research the origin of all the stereotypes, all the cliches, and the prejudices that were gradually constructed about Africa.

The study was based on images. I examined drawings, in particular, pencil drawings found in a French newspaper of that era. I wanted to show how this publication justified the colonization of Africa by defending the French "civilizing mission." The chapter which I examined was titled, "The Civilizing Mission of France." For example, that chapter painted Samory Toure as a bandit and a bloodthirsty king; Behanzin, the king of

Abomey, was presented as the head of a drug-infested, cannibalistic empire. For the French, to carry out their civilizing mission in Africa, it was absolutely necessary to subdue African resistance leaders.

So, [conducting research for my Masters degree] was a turning point for me. The study was that of a history that had preoccupied my mind. When I finished the *maitrise*, I felt compelled to examine this history further by interrogating contemporary reality, especially how all the clichés, stereotypes, and racial prejudices about Africa have been propagated and maintained by contemporary film documentaries.

So, I decided to go to film school to learn the language of cinema, because I needed to understand this medium known as film in order to better elaborate my analysis and my investigation of the perception of Africa held in Western countries.

DB: When did the changes come about?

GK:It was around the time that I completed the Masters, 1973-1974. My first year at film school was 1974-1975. It was also the fifth year of my history studies. When I went to film school it was to learn the technique, the language of film to aid me in the study of history. I was not planning to become a film-maker, but I was learning film because I was hoping to use it in the field of history both in relation to my specific research and also to make archaeological films. I wanted to try to use film to disseminate knowledge about history to the masses. These are a few of the motives, objectives, concerns that I had.

But when I entered film school, I developed a passion for that study, notably the acquisition of cinematographic language, how to write a scenario. I understood that I liked film more than I realized and that it was just as important for me to use film to tell stories as it was to report history. So, I finished film school in two years, 1974-1976, came out with a degree in film production, and returned to my country, which was then known as the Upper Volta. Ordinarily I would have gone to the university to teach history. Instead, I decided to stay with film and to work at the Ministry of Information, the administrative and political headquarters for film activities.

So I launched my career in September 1976. I still taught at the university because a film school, the African Institute for Cinematographic Education, was created over there. I taught technical material involving film, audio-visual technology, and introduction to scenario writing. But I also taught the methodology of documenting the oral tradition, notably the method used by Jean Von Sillon, the history and sociology of African film, as well as other secondary courses in other disciplines. These are some of what brought me to film.

What interested me in history with a capital "H" was, in part, the reconstruction of memory: the need to know from whence one came to better know where one is going. I realized that film would be an important tool for me to achieve that goal, because I could, by way of history with a small "h," try to speak to people about their past, their present, and their future. I believe that was my main motivation in film. In fact, all the films that I have made touch upon this question of belonging, of reconnecting to one's own history, of rediscovering one's roots. For me, it is a major theme, particularly in Africa, in view of our history, both the history of those who remained on the continent, and of those in the diaspora, who were taken away from the continent.

I believe that it is a theme that encompasses all the others. And whatever may be this confirmation, this meeting somewhere, it is always necessary to define oneself, to try, in any case, to understand one's historical experience. That has always fascinated me. I would say that history was the terrain upon which my desire to become a film-maker grew. But it happened without my actually being aware, for at some point the two things came together.

DB:What was your first film?

GK:My first feature film is *Wend Kuuni* which was made in 1981-82.

DB:The first film you ever made.

GK:I made other films.

DB:I would like you to talk about the very first film that you ever made.

GK:The very first film that I made was not actually my film. It was important for me because it was in the framework of my teaching at INAFEC, the African Institute for Cinematographic Education. It was in the framework of my course, "Introduction to Scenario Writing and the Craft of Production," that I and the first class of INAFEC, the acronym for the Institut Africain d'Education Cinématographique (African Institute for Cinematographic Education), chose a topic from those presented by the students.

We developed the subject; there was money that UNESCO gave and we made a film with it. It is called "Je viens de Bokin" ("I Come from Bokin"). I was the pedagogical framer and was involved in the production at the technical and staging levels. That was my first experience with making a film, even though the film was not totally mine. I put everything that I had into it.

I also worked with a young film-maker who was beginning his career and who had the opportunity to involve students in his production. Afterwards, I made a second film, a didactic film about the stocking and conservation of grains. That was entirely my own production. It was a documentary film about the problems farmers encounter when trying to protect harvests from predators, insects, and the like. There was a workshop organized by a West African economic organization and held in Ouagadougou. They provided the money to make the film, which was titled "Stocker et conserver les grains."

Afterwards I made a film about FESPACO 1979, called "Regard sur le 6e FESPACO" (Highlights of the 6th FESPACO). It was in Burkina at FESPACO. One can still obtain a cassette. "Regard sur le 6e FESPACO" was a type of documentary about the 6th FESPACO which was held in 1979 in Ouagadougou. I interviewed several people, journalists and film-makers, about the problems in African film.

Then in October 1981, I began filming *Wend Kuuni*. I had written the scenario in 1979, but I was unable to start filming until 1981. The film took 33 days to make but the 33 days were spread between October 15, 1981 and February 17, 1982. The film was completed around May 18, 1982. It was presented for the first time at the Cannes Film Festival on May 25, 1982. After that, the film was shown at a number of festivals. It was a film that rather rapidly became famous contrary to all expectation because it was my first fiction film. I think that it was the experience that confirmed for me how to make a film that would speak to my people in a profound way, in a language that they can understand, in a narrative that they are accustomed to.

And that's why I wrote *Wend Kuuni* in the form of a traditional tale. I wanted the most popular indigenous narrative mode and cinematographic narrative to mutually fertilize each other, to create something that draws strength from one or the other. I believe that it was rather convincing because the people saw it as an attempt to form a new cinematographic narrative. I stayed with this idea since then. My other films like *Rabi*, the 3rd film that I made in 1982, and *Buud Yam*, my last film, made in 1997, continue to draw their foundation from this cinematographic approach.

And I believe that it's something that allows me to focus on my other objective, memory, that is, collective memory. How is it constructed? How can we go about drawing energy from the knowledge of our past? It is almost an obsession for me, and I believe that all my films, all the subjects that I have, reflect this obsession. I have two or three projects whose scenarios are at different stages of elaboration and revolve around this theme of memory. I recognize that it is a place from which I cannot escape because it is from this theme that I draw the strength to approach my subjects and to try to reach the spectators.

DB: One of the things that I find interesting in *Wend Kuuni* is the theme of the future of women seen through the character Pognere. My students talked about it at length. They enjoyed *Wend Kuuni*, especially the character Pognere. How did you find the actors from *Wend Kuuni*?

GK: The shooting period for *Wend Kuuni*, as I said earlier, was very long. However we only actually filmed for 33 days. I had adapted myself to the children's schedule because they were in school and I didn't want to disturb their studies. So we would film on Thursdays. I found the children around me. At first I looked for children to play the parts. I did a little casting, but finally, I found the children who seemed to fit the roles in my own family. But I had doubts because since they were close to me, I said to myself: "can I be adequately objective and will I be able to distance myself enough from them to get what I want?"

Finally, from the first cuts, when we began filming, my technical crew forced me to keep [the children] because they were so convincing. That brought me a sense of assurance. In final analysis, it was the other collaborators who participated in the final decision to keep the child actors from my family. The other actors, like the father, Tinga is a science teacher. The mother, Lale was working as a secretary in the public sector. But when the film was released the people, even at home, could not tell that they were not peasants. In other words, their acting was exact. It is also their talent for acting which was so tremendous. People asked, "but where did you find that peasant?" I would answer, "but that peasant is not a peasant everyday; it is someone who lives in town."

Also, there were other actors, whom I found in the village to play secondary roles. Whenever I want to choose actors, I first of all recount the scenario to several people, then, I discuss it with them that they might truly internalize the story. In deed, I must say that I was fortunate to have found the two children but also the two parents, the mother and father, Tinga and Lale, because since then, I have always used them.

This means that I met people with whom I share much more than the history of one film. They have become people for whom I have friendship and affection, so much so that when I write my scenarios, it is almost understood that they will play the roles, even though they are not stars. They are people who do not make their living from acting. They have other jobs. They are not professionals actors. When I want to make a film, I go to the village where I shoot most of my films, a village about 35 km from Ouagadougou and I always tell the story that I want to film to everyone, to the elders, the wise men in the village. I realize that while I'm going to tell a fictional story, it is going to interfere with their daily lives.

The film will still be here when they're gone and I do not want the film to lie about the nature of the people. So, this means a very deliberate weaving between reality and fiction. I film their lives, their reality today, but something that happened long ago could happen today. I have had the chance to meet interesting people who understand the work that I'm doing and so I make sure that my camera does not become an intruder into the universe. I do not come as a "peeping tom" to film.

I am aware that I'm entering their lives and that they must authorize me to enter their lives, that they accept me. Today, one can say that in that village cinema has become something natural for them, because I made my first film there in 1981 and have since made three other films there. So, when we arrive we start filming. When we shout "silence," the people stop making noise out of respect for my work, because they understand that this is also a way of prolonging the life of the village. That energizes me a lot. I remember that in commemoration of the cinema centennaire the French TV channel Canal Plus made a film about me. I went to the village. For me, this village is both a place of fiction and of reality. And films are in a way vehicles that go back and forth between reality and fiction in the village.

After each release, I go to show them the film. So, beyond the fictional aspect, the film is also something that becomes a part of their collective memory. That is they feel that they had a part in the cinematographic adventure that I orchestrated. They too have become people who are close to me daily. When there are events there, I go; I also greet everyone when there are deaths, because I have been adopted by the village, like a child of the village. So, there cinema overtakes fiction and becomes part of the present.

DB: A similar problem is presented in Fanta Nacro's film *Un Certain matin* where film-makers go into a village to make a film without informing the residents. It is a very short but interesting piece about cinema as a type of intruder. Now, we come to your film, *Buud Yam*, which won the 1997 Etalon de Yennenga at FESPACO. When you completed *Wend Kuuni* or during the filming, had you already given thought to a sequel? And then would you speak to us about *Buud Yam*. What inspired you? What would you like the spectator to retain?

GK: When I made *Wend Kuuni* I did not film the entire scenario. Let's say that I shot only about 60-70% of the story of *Wend Kuuni* because for a heap of reasons we couldn't do it as I had written it. So I tried to shoot a shorter ending. Therefore, *Wend Kuuni* is 75 minutes long. At the onset we wanted to make a feature film. But in the end, it was an adequate length for the story that I was telling and the film was shown in several countries with that length. It never posed a problem. But when the spectators in Burkina saw the film, they were so touched by the children. They said, "Gaston you must tell the rest of the story. What happened to the children? Are they going to get married? Are they going to remain adopted brother and sister?"

Family members, friends, and unknown spectators began to say, "Oh, there will be a sequel to the film." And besides, what's so strange is that on Sept. 1, 1982 the film opened for the first time at the Ciné Burkina. When I first arrived, people were already in the theater and I tried to enter. The doorman asked for my ticket. I said: "I don't have a ticket." He said to me: "If you don't have a ticket you can't come in." So I told him that I'm the one who made the film. He looked at me suspiciously and he still didn't want to let me in. A manager of the theater came and said to him, "Why yes, it's Gaston Kaboré; he's the one who made the film we're going to show." So the doorman looked me up and down. "Yeah, another scheme," he said. I remember him taking me by the hand, pulling me into the theater as if he couldn't see. So I entered the theater. The film went well. When we came out there were two people in front of me. One of them said "That film was a little short. It was very interesting but short." But the other one said, "No, that's just the first part; there's going to be a sequel." The film no longer belonged to me and the people had decided something against my will.

So I listened to that and then afterwards people said, "You need to do something." I replied, saying, "No. Just because you make a film doesn't mean that there has to be a sequel." I was opposed to that, because it is a practice of commercial film that works well but my film was not built around star actors and all that. I couldn't really see how I could make a sequel to *Wend Kuuni* right away, using the same actors. However, since I had not filmed the whole story of "Wend Kuuni," and because there was that pressure, that demand from the spectators, in 1979, I said to myself, "Seven years have passed since the film was made. What has happened to the characters of my film?" So, I began to investigate the life of my characters as if they really existed and that's how I began to write a scenario, but without telling myself that it was going to turn into a film I wanted to first confirm that I had enough material to tell a strong, beautiful story that generated its own necessity. In 1990, the scenario was completed and I began to look for the money. It took awhile to find the financial backing, but it produced *Buud Yam*.

DB: What does "Buud Yam" mean?

GK: "Buud Yam" is not easy to translate because it is composed of two words. The first word when used alone is pronounced "budu" in More which is the language spoken in the film. "Budu" means seed, the grain that one puts in the ground. It also means the ancestors, one's lineage, the people from whom you originate. And it also means descendants, the generations that come after you.

So it means, simultaneously, belonging and identity. It also suggests heritage, the legacy that one is going to leave to others. And the second word "yam" means simultaneously, intelligence, behavior, and memory, the capacity to retain things. So the two words together could mean the desire for roots and the desire to transmit. That's why I did not try to translate the term into a language other than More, because it would have become some grand phrase. When I wrote the script for *Buud Yam* evidently I wanted there to be a connection with "Wend Kuuni." No matter how I defend myself, *Buud Yam* is still a sequel. But it's not an immediate sequel. One can view *Buud Yam* and understand it without ever having seen "Wend Kuuni."

The scripting took a long time, and even when I finished the film script and found the money, I continued to write. For me, *Buud Yam* had to be a deepening of everything that I had tried to do in "Wend Kuuni." And that's how I, slowly, constructed a story that is still based on the relationship between the two children who have become young people, and who are at a turning point in their lives, when the adopted sister has great affection for her adopted brother. That's why the story of *Wend Kuuni* and of *Buud Yam* is, somewhat, the story of Pognere's growing feelings for her brother. The illness that has overtaken her is psychosomatic. It is the physical manifestation of the inner hurt that is gnawing at Wend Kuuni who suffers from never having known his father. So it's a type of inner pain in regards to his identity.

So, somehow, Pognere's enigmatic dream is a manifestation of Wend Kuuni's search, and, in some way, she had to fall ill so that he would undertake the journey that might free him of the inner turmoil which he has been experiencing. Consequently, he officially goes in search of a healer to save his sister. But internally, his quest is a search for identity, because one is always the son of someone or the daughter of someone; it's something fundamental, even if one doesn't think about it everyday. It's something basic to the human personality. But, *Wend Kuuni* had not yet resolved that problem. Pognere's illness makes him travel through time and space in search of a healer. But while searching for the healer for his sister he is also going to heal himself. When the film ends, *Wend Kuuni* understands that in actuality the voyage was even more important for him than it was for his sister and that there remains another voyage to make. So this voyage, is it going to be again spatial and physical or more of an inner excursion into his memory. I am waiting for him to tell me and then perhaps I could tell the spectator.

DB: A voyage of initiation. One last question. How did it feel to receive the Etalon de Yennenga? What was your reaction when you were announced the winner of the coveted prize? What has it meant for your career?

GK: It brings pleasure. One is happy when one receives a distinction, to be credited by a festival like FESPACO, to have made the best film in the competition. I think it's something that merits its golden moment. It's first of all, the joy of having made a film that is liked by the public and judged by the jury to be the best in a competition. The Etalon is an important label because it's rare that one receives it twice. At any rate the history of the festival shows that only one person has won the prize twice. Truly it's joining the stars. A prize is something that could or could not be won. It's tied to few things.

If the film had come out a year earlier or a year later, it may not have had the same impact on the public and the jury. So, one must understand that it's something that's very "aller à l'etoile." At the same time, when it does happen, it's very important. For me, I think [the prize] was a type of recognition for the work that I try to do, the struggle that I have waged in order to invent a language of our own cinema, and for saying that we must find in our own land, in our history, the inspiration and the narrative forms to make films. *Buud Yam* is my fourth film. To me, in terms of style, scenario, and technical difficulty in production, it is my most accomplished film. So I am happy for all these reasons and think that the Etalon is going to have an impact on the commercial and cultural success of the film. It's certain that the prize is a stop sign that calls people's attention to the film, and I hope that is going to help me to make a fifth feature film.

But what pleases me most is the closeness between the popular reception impact of the film and the jury selection. Since the festival ended, we have already made nearly 40,000 entries for the film *Buud Yam*. Each time that it's shown, the theaters are full, and I would say that this distribution which has had box office success brings me as much pleasure as having received the Etalon de Yennenga.

DB: Gaston, thank you.

* * *

Gaston Jean-Marie Kabore was born in Bobo-Dioulasso, Upper Volta (now Burkina Faso) in 1951. Kabore completed the French *licence* and the *Maitrise* in history at the Sorbonne in Paris before beginning his film studies. Shortly after his return to his country, Burkina Faso, he was appointed technical adviser in charge of cinema at the Ministry of Information and Culture (1977-1981); Director of the National Cinema Centre (1977-1988); teacher at INAFEC [L'Institut Africain d'Education Cinématographique] (1977-1986); member of the FESPACO Organizing Committee since 1978. He served as President of FEPACI [Fédération Panafricaine des Cinéastes] for ten years; member of the Board of Directors of the Foundation and Chairman of the "Training and Technical Assistance" Commission; "Chevalier des Arts et des Lettres des Ordres Français, Commandeur de l'Ordre National." He has produced sixteen films including, *Je viens de Bokin* (1977), *Stockez et conservez les grains* (1978), *Regard sur le sixième FESPACO* (1979), *Wend Kuuni* (1982), *Rabi* (1982), *Buud Yam* (1986), and *Zan Boko* (1988). Kaboré's student, Idrissa Ouédraogo, won the Étalon de Yennenga in 1981 with his film *Tilaï.*

The interview took place at the 23rd Annual Conference of the African Literature Association, "FESPACO Nights in Michigan," on the campus of Michigan State University, April 19, 1997

5

NGOZI ONWURAH INTERVIEWED

by Maureen Eke

Nigerian-born Black British film maker, Ngozi Onwurah has made over twenty films, some of which include *Monday's Girls*, *The Body Beautiful*, and *I Bring You Frankincense*. This interview took place at the African Literature Association conference, "FESPACO Nights in Michigan" on April 20, 1997.

EKE: Ngozi, could you tell us something about yourself and how you came to make films.

ONWURAH: I was born in England and went to live in Nigeria when I was two. My father is Nigerian; my mother is English, white English of Irish stock. When I was about twelve, my father left us and we came back to England with my younger brother and younger sister and we went back to our mother's home town of New Castle. It was an important time in my life. It was a completely white city. They had never seen any black people before. So, we went from being African children growing up in a completely African environment, one day, to London, a completely white world, the next day. This has informed a lot of my filmmaking.

How I came to filmmaking? I actually wanted to be a writer; I thought I want to become a writer. Anyone who knows something about Africa knows that there is a lot of storytelling tradition, lots of storytelling; everything gets turned into a story. When I came to England, I was so miserable. I used to spend all my time reading books or watching TV and losing myself in those worlds. So, I thought I wanted to be a writer. But as I grew up, it became obvious to me that filmmaking was the modern form of storytelling. So, it was logical that I became interested in filmmaking and went to film school. I did a post-graduate work in film and then started working professionally.

EKE: What social ideas or ideologies determine the types of films you make?

ONWURAH: I am not a political animal, and I don't like making films about issues. But, obviously, because of who I am and how I grew up, which is basically that when you are in Africa, you don't know whether you are black. You are Igbo or just whatever you are, and then you arrive in England, and suddenly, nobody wants to be your friend. People call you names. You are different. People laugh at you. You slowly realize that it is because you are black. And, then, you become black. To me at the age of twelve, basically, I was always the outsider.

In New Castle, I was considered a being nobody wanted to sit next to. I left New Castle when I was about fifteen or sixteen. I hated [New Castle] so much. My mother allowed me to move to Manchester, which was much more multiracial, to go to sixth form college there, because she knew that I was going to run away without her knowing it. When I got to Manchester, it was just in the post-rock period when black was hip because of reggae, because of music, and all these white boys and girls wanted black friends. So, I went from being really, really unpopular to the most popular person on the block. By then, it was too late. I had become intrinsically alone and an outsider, except this time, I could belong if I wanted to. So, I think it has always informed my film making. I am always on the outside, looking in, watching what people are doing. I tend to be more interested in black stories than in the white stories.

EKE: You've mentioned some of the themes: the issue of identity and black stories that interest you. Are there any other topics that you like to pursue in your films?

ONWURAH: Obviously, the Black stories. I also tend to live in the stories for some reason. I am also interested in the visual, especially, with its interplay with the black aesthetics. You can do a lot of juxtapositioning because there is very little, or it is so stereotypical, of what you see black people doing on the screen. You can play with that or you can make a visual statement with that. For instance in *The Body Beautiful* when you see this elderly or older white woman with her one breast missing and rheumatoid arthritis all over her body making love to this very young, virile, black guy, who obviously works out, there is a whole lot of things that you are playing around with through the images.

If you didn't know exactly . . . you might say it is a shot of just an older woman with a younger man. But there is a lot else going on. She's supposed to have an ugly body and he is a black man who is supposed to be virile. You can play a lot more, much broader with the image. It might be with a white man, but there is less room to play with as far as I am concerned.

EKE: Are there any particular messages that you hope to communicate through your films?

ONWURAH: There is a very obvious point in terms of black humanity. It seems so ridiculous that in this day and age we are still reinforcing the fact that black people have humanity. Obviously, that is an important point. At one point, I used to think that what I wanted to do was make white people care about us, so that if they looked at the screen and saw our stories and realized what happened to us, they could care about us. But, actually, I think now that it is more imperative that black people care about black people, because there is a lot of problems going on in [black communities]. Also, I am tired of white stories. I think that Woody Allen angst films are being told over and over again, that Rambo's sieges on earth are being told over and over again. I think black stories and other stories would actually excite people.

What I think our stories will do is remind white people that they have a humanity because I think white stories are getting less and less human. [Now], they are all about volcanoes, earthquakes, and people from out of space. They just regurgitate themselves, whereas we have stories about thirteen year olds who run off into the fields to join the ANC to fight for their country, or stories about black women. Our stories haven't been told. So, we can now remind others of black humanity.

EKE: In fact, as you talk about the telling of these stories, it makes me think about your audience. It seems to me that as you tell particular stories or look at these particular issues, the stories or the films are, therefore, directed at a certain audience. Is there a specific audience that you address in your films or do you simple direct your films at a global audience?

ONWURAH: I think for a film maker, any time a film is watched, the more people who watch and relate to it, the better. In the end, we are all human beings, and if your films can reach everybody, then you have really succeeded. So, as a film maker, I want my films to reach as many people as possible. But, as a film maker, I feel that the audience that I am answerable to is a black audience. So, I want whites, Chinese . . . I want everybody: right wing, left wing . . . to watch my films and get something from them.

But in terms of whom I feel I am answerable to as an audience, I think I am answerable to definitely a black audience, and even beyond that, specifically, a black non-intellectual audience. I don't mean that they are a stupid audience. But, I think academics and intellectuals have very much different perspectives in terms of watching films. So, if that audience turns around and says to me, "You've got this wrong," or asks, "Why did you do that?", I feel that I have to answer those questions. If a white audience turns around to me and asks, "Why did you do that? I think it is wrong," I feel that's its opinion and I have my opinion. I don't feel that I am answerable to a white audience in the same way that I am answerable to a black audience.

EKE: That is quite interesting. As a female or woman film maker, and more specifically, as a Nigerian film maker, what are some of the problems you've encountered while making films, distributing them, or even, in the way people have perceived your films?

ONWURAH: It is really a difficult question to answer, because I've done such a [wide] range of films. Obviously, with the films I've done for the Hong Kong/British Television, there is no problem because there are very few black characters in them. I do mainstream television and in mainstream TV, I get paid very well. I have a lot of resources and a big crew, good schedule, but then, story lines are [approved] by a committee. "Poppy," the last TV series I did, got nineteen million viewers which is sixty-four percent of the market share. So, they [mainstream TV] don't take risks. You can't. You've got to shoot [the film] in a certain way. A little bit of playing around is allowed, but not a lot. There are hardly any black characters in it.

Then, when I am doing independent dramas, short dramas, which usually do have a black story line, the budgets are very low, because they say it is a minority audience I'm dealing with. So, they don't give you a big budget. And, when you're doing drama—drama is very expensive—you've got to improvise and what you find yourself doing is that you end up exploiting black people because you get on the phone and you say: "Look, I know you're an actor. I know you've trained for ten years. I know you're really experienced. Will you do this for me for ten pounds a day?" Or, you ring up a black art director or a black patron. You just find out that what's happened is that the white institution has given you little money for this. So, instead of them directly exploiting black people, they can get a black person to go and exploit black people.

So, morally, it is very dirty. On the other hand, we can say that we are all adults. We do this out of our own choice. My friends who are actors and who direct a little, don't do this any more. I am asking them to do it. But in a way they do have to do it because they do have to get experience. So, we become a cheap training ground. Morally, it is very problematic. And as much as you don't feel alright because there is not enough money to make the film, or say, "I am not going to do it unless I can pay people properly," there is no film at the end of the day. So, nobody gets to see anything;

nobody gets any experience. Or, do you accept your position as a kind of middle man until we make the best film we can? Hopefully, that will lead to something. The problem is that usually it doesn't. People look at a CV and see it is filled with black films; they think affirmative action; they think discrimination; they think it is a substandard form. That's very complicated.

Then you have documentaries. If you're making documentaries overseas, for instance, in Nigeria, you have to bring the whole crew from England to Africa. If you want it in time, use indigenous people to make the film. You have the problem of a different level of experience, a different level of broadcast standards. The BBC will not broadcast "out-of-focus" shots. But in a country like Nigeria, Nigerian TV will broadcast anything. A lot of people don't realize that what they get to broadcast on Nigerian TV is not broadcastable in any other part of the world. I can't even begin to tell you the problems of being a black film maker.

EKE: One of your popular films here in the United States is *Monday's Girls*. And as you've noticed from the response to it at this conference, it is becoming a popular film to show about women in Nigeria. What do you have to say to any audience that watches *Monday's Girls*? I know that when I've shown the film, the issue of female genital mutilation comes up, no matter how much one tries to point out that the film is not about that (FGM). Can you address this issue of FGM in relation to *Monday's Girls*?

ONWURAH: It completely horrifies me. It drives me mad when I think about the form of racism that is going on. The film is about a female ceremony. And when you say ceremony, what you have to realize is that the West has all types of ceremonies, but they call them different things. It is the equivalent of young girls going and hanging out at the mall. And, at the period they're hanging out, they start to notice how to get the boys. They're not formal in the West any more, these ceremonies. I made this film about African women coming of age. In America, I am horrified that about 95% of the American female audience watching it thinks that this ceremony is about female circumcision. At no time has circumcision ever been mentioned; at no time has it ever been implied that this is what is happening. But they have a fixed mind now that all black men go around giving their daughters up to other black men to check out their genitals.

It has become a white feminist issue. I've never been very fond of white feminism. From a long time ago, [the Onwurahs] have been involved with the ANC. Because my father studied in England, he met a lot of the South African exiles. He is an African man. So, we've always been part of the ANC. The feminist movement of the sixties and seventies spent a lot of time and effort trying to raise money to set up family planning and abortion clinics in South Africa. The women in the ANC spent a lot of time trying to explain to these white women that they really didn't need to bother, that the problem the African women had in South Africa was giving birth safely and these children living. So, they spent a lot of money giving ante-natal classes. This wasn't a feminist agenda. The feminist agenda was about contraception and abortion rights, even if they were completely out of context for black women.

And, it is similar with this film. It is similar in the approach now with circumcision as something horrific to [white feminists], even though there is no chance of that ever happening to [the black girls in *Monday's Girls*]. They [feminists] have found out that [circumcision] happened in certain areas of Africa, and they have decided that this shows how barbaric men are, how barbaric African men are, and how this is the priority for all African women. The fact that we don't have universal health care, the fact that more women die in childbirth than will ever die in circumcision rituals are all irrelevant. It is not about how many women they can help in the African continent. It is about what's been horrifying to them the most, what's been least appealing to them, and what they can do about that. I think they think I am a liar when I stand up before them and say that in this part of Nigeria, female circumcision is extremely rare; it is not a tradition. These girls definitely are not doing it.

So, I have responses like: "Well, was there anything that Monday Moses wouldn't let you film?" Yes. There are certain things. I couldn't follow her into the toilet. I couldn't watch her having a bath. They actually think I am lying. But the [they] wouldn't if some white director stood up and said something. They would believe her. If female circumcision happens, it is terrible. I don't think it should happen. I think, though, that it is for the people of the continent to decide a lot of things as well. I think Westerners' role should never get beyond education, provide education and let the people on the ground make their own choices.

EKE: Thank you, Ngozi. Could you now mention some of your other films? I know you have others, including *The Body Beautiful*. I also think that a lot of people do not know about the other films you have made.

ONWURAH: I made a film called *And Still I Rise* which is about black women's sexuality and how people have viewed black women over the last four or three hundred years, or since missionaries first came into contact with them. I've made a film called *Who Stole the Show*. I've done a film called *Flight of the Swan* about a young girl who came from Africa to England. She wants to be a ballerina and is a very good dancer. But she can not be a ballerina, because at that time, English ballet schools had a philosophy that black girls couldn't become ballerinas till they've mastered the symmetry of "cours de ballet." But, she has an African spirit that comes with her and [the film] ends with this beautiful scene of [the girl] dancing the part of the swan in "Swan Lake," and she starts to fly.

I've done a drama called *White men Are Cracking Up*. As a mixed-race woman, I am always aware of how white men view me. I am much more attractive to them than I really am, in terms of being exotic. And so, this woman [in the film] utilizes the power that she has over older white established men to encourage them to commit suicide. That's her way of getting rid of a lot of powerful old men who have nothing to live for any more except their fantasies about her. I've made a film called *Behind the Mask* which is about the last sovereign Oba of Benin and the Benin bronzes and how they ended up in museums [outside Nigeria]. There are more of those Benin bronzes in Germany, America, and Britain than there are in Nigeria.

My last film is called *I Bring You Frankincense* and is about a little mixed-race boy growing up with his white mother in a village outside London. London is full of white people. Every year, he plays the dark wise man; there are three wise men in the Nativity play, and he is always the dark wise man who has to always say, "I bring you frankincense." He thinks Marvin Gaye is his dad because that is the only black person he's ever seen on TV.

EKE: This is wonderful. It is a mixed catalog of films to see. You mentioned that California Newsreel distributes *Monday's Girls* and Women Make Movies distributes your other films. What has been the reception of your films in the West in comparison to Africa, and more specifically, to Nigeria?

ONWURAH: As you know there really is not a distribution network set up in Africa. When I show my films in Nigeria, I show them to my family. My uncle who lives in Lagos gets some people together and shows my films to them. The interesting thing is that *Monday's Girls* has never been bought by anybody, any university in Nigeria. I think it is because for them, this film is for Europeans. *Monday's Girls* is for Europeans to watch what we're like. Whereas in the old days these films were made by white people and had even more of a European gaze, *Monday's Girls* is made by a black Nigerian woman director. So, there is less of a European gaze on those women. It is still made for European consumption; it is not what Nigerians are particularly interested in. It is not interesting to them. There are lots of films on initiation ceremonies of young Africans. But the Benin bronze one is virtually in every university in Nigeria. It was screened on Nigerian independence day all around Africa. It has been seen in Zimbabwe, Kenya.

The Body Beautiful is like that. It is one of the most successful films I've done critically. It's won just about everything. In Nigeria, they won't get past the fact that I've shown an older woman naked and she's kissing a young man. This is something near pornography and there's a cultural barrier there. Another film which I didn't mention, which is my feature film, is *Welcome II the Terrordome*. There is a lot of violence in it, and it is about the black existence. It is set in a place that's meant to be a cross between Soweto, Brixton, and South Central in L.A. So, it is basically a black ghetto, and there is a lot of violence in it. In Nigeria, it goes down really well because there's a lot of action, a lot of music; it's very loud.

But, the elders, my father's generation can not get past the fact that these kids are being offered free education at school and they are not going to school. You know in [some parts of] Africa, people carry their desks to school; they work hard; everybody wants to go to school and you pay to go. The idea that in America, there are all these black people who could go to school for nothing, or who are saying school is not good enough or "I'd rather do this or that," is just actually quite incomprehensible. My father says that when he went to the university in England, and when he first qualified as a doctor, white women wouldn't let him touch them. They were not going to have this black man examine them. But he kept doing it.

There is a saying that my father says is Nigerian, which is: "may your road be rough." It is the idea that nothing comes to you easily, and, so, if you want a good life, a successful life, your work needs to be rough so that you can earn it. That's not how they think in America. If you said to somebody, "may your road be rough," they'll think you're wishing them ill. Whereas you're saying, "I hope you have lots of obstacles which you can overcome so that you can get something" . . .

EKE: And, it will be worthwhile when you gain it.

ONWURAH: And, it would mean something when you gain it. Whereas, if someone just gives it to you, it doesn't mean anything. I think these are cultural differences that exist between black Americans and African Africans. And, even more literally in-between African Americans and African Africans who are black British. African Africans and African Americans want to bond, want to put their arms around each other. But there are these huge cultural gaps between them and in [*Welcome II the Terrordome*]. I am really interested in these spaces. Those are the missing links that you need to talk about to get people together.

EKE: Thank you very much. This has been a wonderful and informative interview.

Section 3

FILM CTRITICISM

6

THE SUBALTERN SPEAKS:
Remaking/Her/Story in Assia Djebar's
La Nouba des femmes du mont Chenoua

by Touria Khannous

Postcolonial studies have often examined visual representations of the female Arab and African 'other' by Western filmmakers and critics. The publicity given nowadays in the French media to the situation of Algerian women, for instance, demonstrates the inseparability of visual representations and the female migrant body. The media reports on the patriarchal, paternalistic attitudes among Algerian families and on the problematic of the veil indicate that French culture apprehends the gendered subaltern mainly through metaphors of photographic technology. The French media, however, is implicated in the violence it reports, for it silences the Algerian woman at the same time that it claims to defend her human rights. The Algerian woman is projected in the French media—in the visual texts, the headlines and the photographs—as a victim of both patriarchy and colonialism. Such journalistic accounts merely accentuate the instrumental positioning of these women, who are used as vessels of one kind of patriarchal culture on the one hand and as tools for the imperialist spreading of another (Western) kind of patriarchy on the other hand. The question here is, how is it possible for us to identify the political effects or voices of this subaltern figure herself?

With regard to cinema, little has been produced about the cultural reality and history of the Algerian woman in French cinematic discourse. French film critics such as Pierre Jeancolas have pointed out the silence that characterizes French cinema, in general, on the country's colonial history and its relationship to its former colonies.[1] French films which centered on the colonies were often saturated with imperialist representations that often reduced the native population to an absence. The colonial history of Algeria, in particular, has not been openly addressed in French cinema. In her introduction to *Cinema, Colonialism, Postcolonialism*, Dina Sherzer argues that the few French films which were produced in the 1960's dealt with the Franco-Algerian colonial past only in a subliminal way.[2] Sherzer cites French filmmaker Alain Resnais' two films *Last Year in Marienbad* and *Muriel*, in which Resnais refers only in a roundabout way to the crimes which were committed by the French in Algeria. The conflation between the Algerian woman and the Algerian nation figures in both films, in scenes that portray rape to symbolize the French invasion of Algeria. Such films often misrepresented Algerian women and ignored their agency and their active participation during the war of liberation.

It was in the famous Italian-Algerian *Battle of Algiers* (1966) by Gillo Pontecorco that Algerian women were given credit for their active participation during the war. This film, which presents events from the Algerian point of view, represents Algerian women as active agents during the revolution. In this film, women used their bodies as weapons of war. They unveiled themselves in order to smuggle arms past the French guards, acted as liaisons between the male nationalist heroes and carried bombs. Masqueraded as European women, the Algerian women in the film carried explosives in their handbags and navigated the streets of Algiers in their resistance to colonial domination. The film also demonstrates how in addition to masquerade, Algerian women hid bombs, guns and grenades under their veils, once the French soldiers started to realize that they were posing as European women.

While *Battle of Algiers* has been praised for its representation of Algerian women's role in the national struggle, it has also been criticized for ignoring their other struggle, the one against patriarchy.[3] The issue of Algerian women's social emancipation has been elided and subordinated, obviously, to national struggle and liberation in the film. Femininity as commodity and spectacle also figures in *Battle of Algiers*, where the masqueraded Algerian women are represented as objects of the French soldiers' erotic looking. What is also obvious to the female spectator is the absence of the Algerian woman's perspective or of any identifiable female voice concerning anti-colonial struggle in this director's visual representations of decolonization, resistance and colonial war. The film reinscribes the same device of 'othering,' that was characteristic of French cinema's representation of Algerian women. The conflation of the nation and the Algerian woman which is characteristic of French colonial films also figures here, as illustrated in the final images of an Algerian woman holding the Algerian flag. This kind of representation of Algerian women in both French and Algerian cinema is the result of a history that has ignored the presence of Algerian women in the political scene.

My aim in this paper is to explore another aspect of postcolonial Algerian film by offering an analysis of *La Nouba des femmes du Mont Chenoua,*[4] in which Assia Djebar gives the audience her own representation of colonialism and Algerian women's culture. To film *La Nouba,* Assia Djebar went back to the mountain of Chenoua in order to speak to peasant women in her tribe and to listen to the stories of their own experiences during the war. In the narrative, Lila, the filmmaker's "alter-ego," returns to the tribal village of Cherchell in search of testimonial proof of her brother's disappearance during the war. She is accompanied by her husband, Ali, who is mute and paralyzed, as a result of falling from a horse, and her daughter Aicha. Lila is introduced in the narrative as inhabiting a "home" space in which she is experiencing some discomfort as a result of her husband's paralysis. Thus, much of her time is spent outside, in her car, and in other Algerian women's houses. The film is a mixture of documentary, fiction, oral history, and music as well as multiple cultural codes and languages. Its heterogeneous references are made crystal clear in its multiple dedications, first to the Hungarian musician Bela Bartok, who came to the "silenced Algeria" in 1913 to study popular music, and second to the Algerian warrior Zouleikha, who, in 1955 and 1956, coordinated national resistance in both the city and the mountains of Cherchell. The audience is told in the dedication that Lila, the film's protagonist, could be the daughter of Zouleikha. The other six women of Chenoua who "speak" tell some fragments of their real history. The introduction to the film defines "La Nouba des Femmes" as "histoire des femmes (qui parlent "a leur tour") [History of women who speak in their turn].[5] "Nouba" in Arabic, the audience is told, signifies a type of symphony in classical music, called "Andalousian music," with certain specific rhythmic movements. In the Algerian and Moroccan dialects, "Nouba" means "turn." The film, as its title indicates, blends Algerian women's speech and history with musical fragments, and French with Arabic.

A Feminist Film?

Djebar has commented upon the filming of *La Nouba* in interviews as well as in the seven chapters entitled "Femme Arabe" [Arab Woman] in her recent novel *Vaste est la prison* (1995). In speaking about one of the characters of the film, Djebar states: "Je suis ravie. Ferial est la première non seulement à jouer les vedettes, mais à pratiquer du "féminisme" à sa manière. Ton film, c'est sur les femmes? me demande-t-elle. Bien sur, je dis" [I am pleased. Feriel is the first one not only to play the role of a star, but also to practice feminism in her own way. Your film, is it on women? she asked me. Of course, I said] (247). In an another interview, Djebar asserts that there is more to her film than its focus on women: "To say that my film is a film about women is meaningless. I will always be drawn to making films.... Women's bodies, women, are my subject matter. It's a little like being a sculptor: one uses one material, another a different material" (Interview 64). *La Nouba* is explicitly feminist if we take into account Djebar's intention to subvert women's subordination in the contexts of patriarchy and colonialism,[6] but it is also the aesthetic aspect of the film which Djebar reminds the viewer not to ignore.

La Nouba is a good example of feminist "cinematic counter-telling"[7] which characterizes contemporary films produced by Third World women directors. In her essay "Post-Third-Worldist Culture: Gender, Nation, and the Cinema," Ella Shohat states that:

> Third-World feminists, for their part, have participated in these counternarratives, while insisting that colonialism and national resistance have impinged differently on men and women, and that remapping and renaming is not without its fissures and contradictions. (183)

Revolution is, according to Shohat, a recurrent trope in Third World films by women, since it is essential for their feminist projects. "Third-World feminist histories" she asserts, "can be understood as feminist if seen in conjunction with the resistance work these women have performed within their communities and nations. Any serious discussion of feminist cinema must therefore engage the complex question of the 'national'" (186). Thus, it would be misleading to read film in a language devoted to its aesthetic aspects while depriving it of its political and feminist overtones, for "post-Third-Worldist feminist films and videos conduct a struggle on two fronts, at once aesthetic and political, synthesizing revisionist historiography with formal innovation" (188). *La Nouba* was obviously done with a conscious feminist and political sensibility, for it captures the voices of women who shared in the making of Algerian history and culture.

In her book, *Femmes Fatales; Feminism, Film Theory, Psychoanalysis* (1991), Mary Anne Doane has argued that contemporary feminist film practice "addresses itself to the activity of uncoding, de-coding, deconstructing the given images. It is a project of defamiliarization whose aim is not necessarily that of seeing the female body differently, but of exposing the habitual meanings/values attached to femininity as cultural constructions" (Doane 166). Djebar engages what Doane suggests, in her deconstructions of cultural constructions of femininity in her film. What distinguishes her feminist project from Western feminist film practice, however, is its de/construction of Algerian women's given images in both patriarchy and colonialism. While Djebar's project evokes First world feminist film practice in its de-coding of the cultural constructions of gender, it allies itself primarily with Third world feminist filmmaking because of the specificity of its ethnic and national positions. The film is clearly marked by nationalist and revolutionary agendas, and it highlights an Algerian feminism centered on the female collective. The film's feminist and political agenda can be examined only through an exploration of its subversive poetics as well as its multiple interventions in the ideologies of modern Algerian history. In what follows, I examine *La Nouba* 's multiple interventions in the ideologies of colonialism and patriarchy through a discussion of female speech, the female gaze, female space, language, translation and (female) history as materialized in the film.

The Subaltern speaks

Djebar's project resonates with current themes in post-colonial theory and subaltern studies, for it evokes familiar questions concerning the problematic of language, the history of Algeria, and the question of the subaltern. Djebar's representation of Algerian women's speech, for instance, seems to engage Gayatri Spivak's take on subalternity and speech in her essay "Can the Subaltern Speak?" Spivak argues in this essay about the double effacement of women in the history of the subaltern; as she puts it: "...both as object of colonialist historiography and as subject of insurgency, the ideological construction of gender keeps the male dominant. If, in the context of colonial production, the subaltern has no history and cannot speak, the subaltern as female is even more deeply in shadow" (Spivak 287).

Spivak has emphasized the effacement of the Subaltern woman by asking the question "Can she speak?" and she answers the question in the negative. In order for us to understand Spivak's claim that "the subaltern cannot speak," we first need to examine the story about Bhuvaneswari Bhaduri's suicide which has led to her conclusion. Her story as written by Spivak is as follows:

> A young woman of sixteen or seventeen, Bhuvaneswari Bhaduri, hanged herself in her father's modest apartment in North Calcutta in 1926. The suicide was a puzzle since, as Bhuvaneswari was menstruating at the time, it

was clearly not a case of illicit pregnancy. Nearly a decade later, it was discovered that she was a member of one of the many groups involved in the armed struggle for Indian independence. She had finally been entrusted with a political assassination. Unable to confront the task and yet aware of the practical need for trust, she killed herself. (307)

Commenting on Bhuvaneswari's suicide, Spivak states that "the subaltern as female cannot be heard or read" (308). According to her, even the letter which Bhuvaneswari left could not reproduce her as a speaking subject. Spivak has explained in an interview that even after the letter in which Bhuvaneswari explained the reasons behind her suicide was discovered, the women in the family decided to forget (Winant 89). Spivak's implication is that within certain discourses of representation, there is no space from which the gendered subaltern can speak. The subaltern woman, Spivak also implies, cannot speak in the place where she is subalternized, but this does not preclude her ability to speak in other contexts for herself.

Djebar poses similar questions concerning the Algerian gendered subaltern: Can she speak? Can she gaze? Can she be in Algeria's history? Assia Djebar is originally from Algeria and is now a professor of French at Louisiana State University. Her own position as a Westernized Algerian woman who has lived in France and now in the United States puts into question her act of representation. *La Nouba*, however, makes evident the ways in which Djebar marks the possibility as well as the limits of her representation. The film highlights the subaltern Algerian woman's speech in the texts of anti-imperialism and nationalism, as well as in the social field.

Throughout the film, Lila, the French-educated daughter of the tribe, voices her intention to listen to the voices of the women of Chenoua: "Je ne cherche rien. Je me souviens seulement que je cherchais. Je ne cherche rien, mais j'écoute. Pour vous, que je voudrais écouter" [I am not looking for anything. I just remembered that I was looking. I am not looking for anything, but I listen. It is for you that I would like to listen]. She also describes the silent manner in which she interacts with these women: "Voici que je commence à vous entendre. Vous, les dames de mon Chenoua. Ouvrir une porte, saluer, ne rien dire, laisser parler. Est-ce le passé, est-ce le présent alors qui me reviens?" [I am beginning to listen to you. You, the women of my Chenoua. Open a door, greet, say nothing, let them speak. Is it the past, or the present which is coming back to me?]. The act of listening to the subaltern speak in Djebar's film enacts Spivak's assertion at the end of her essay that "representation has not withered away" and that "the female intellectual as intellectual has a circumscribed task which she must not disown with a flourish" (308). The act of listening highlights the necessary limits of Djebar's task of her representation of the subaltern Algerian woman, who can only speak in her own language and in her own space. Lila who "would like to listen" to the subaltern woman's speech is hesitant about her ability to listen. This underlines Djebar's anxiety over representation and her awareness of the near impossibility of even the act of listening and the interpretation of what the listener hears, within the discourse of the representation of the subaltern.

Through Lila's act of listening, *La Nouba* succeeds powerfully in capturing the complexity of the Algerian woman's memory by recording her Arabic speech and transcribing it into French. The peasant woman's story about the land which the "gawri" (the Christian man) lent to her, for instance, and which she cultivated herself, is in turn subtitled in French. Lila's voice-over in French carries on with the peasant woman's Arabic speech; it is as if Algerian women must negotiate a specific code of languages in the process of their liberation. All of the women who speak in the film are uneducated Algerian women. The film literally lets them speak. Their speech is embodied just as much in their painful expressions, their anguished tone, and their tears. The film highlights the Algerian woman's speech through the female gaze, female space, the female body, orality and these women's political agency during the war of liberation.

Can the Subaltern gaze?

Djebar's representation of the gaze of the Algerian woman in *La Nouba* resonates with her later critiques of the controlling patriarchal and colonial gaze in the visual representations of Algerian women. In the postface of *Women of Algiers in their Apartment,* Djebar draws a comparison between Delacroix's painting "Femmes d'Alger dans leurs Apartments" and Picasso's series of lithographs and canvasses which carry the same title. In comparing the two starkly different artistic renderings of Algerian women by these two artists, Djebar is getting at the heart of the disparity between how these women are represented in these paintings, and how they would like to represent themselves. Delacroix represents the "colonial night" into which these Algerian women are thrust. His privileged glimpse into the harem is associated with the French imperial intrusion into Algeria. By stealing the "forbidden gaze" at these women, Delacroix is characterized as "the thief, the spy, the voyeur" (137). Delacroix's "orientalizing look" objectifies Algerian women and represents them as oppressed, silent, enclosed, carrying the "perfume of evil haunts" (149).

Notably, it takes an artist who is not French to liberate these women in his work. Picasso's "Spanish genius" "reverses the malediction" (149), as he fills his depiction of Algerian women with light and "the improvised bursting out into an open space" (149). In Picasso's painting, there is a "glorious liberation of space, the bodies awakening in dance, in a flowing outward, the movement freely offered" (149). The narrator marvels at Picasso's ability to capture women of Algiers during the revolution. Picasso's women are unmistakably more free than are Delacroix's, as symbolized by the "denuding" (to represent the unveiling that was occurring at the time of the revolution). Djebar abhors the orientalizing gaze of the colonizer, as exemplified by Delcaroix's painting, as well as the controlling gaze of patriarchy in Algeria. She laments the double imprisonment of Algerian women, and longs for an 'unveiling' which allows Algerian women to move, to look, and to speak for themselves.

La Nouba negates the controlling orientalist and patriarchal gaze by centralizing the female look as an opposition to the male gaze, and as a form of the female collective. The film emphasizes the female collective through the exchange of gazes between Lila and the other Algerian women. Much work in the field of film criticism has been devoted to the idea of the "gaze," and many theories formulated about it have emphasized the scopic drive which propels the male gaze. Enunciation is commonly defined as the filmmaker's desire via the organization of the structure of looking in his/her film as articulated to the spectator and as it engages the spectator's voyeurism.[8] One of the most authoritative texts on the discourse of the gaze is Laura Mulvey's essay "Visual Pleasure and Narrative Cinema," in which she argues that "Unchallenged, mainstream film coded the erotic into the language of the dominant patriarchal order" (16) and that "Woman displayed as sexual object is the leitmotif of erotic spectacle:...she holds the look, and plays to and signifies male desire" (19). Mulvey's main argument in this essay is that narrative film has manipulated visual pleasure in such a way that reproduces a pattern of male looking and female "to-be-looked-at-ness." She contends that feminist cinema necessitates the subversion of this visual pleasure, whereby woman is reproduced as an erotic object for the male hero and the male spectator.

The centrality of Lila's gaze in *La Nouba* is subversive of the voyeuristic visual pleasure which characterizes narrative cinema. The image of Ali, the paralyzed and mute husband, who is confined to his wheelchair inside the house, is juxtaposed to the image of Lila, who is in constant movement in the "Kharidj" [the outside] throughout the film. The camera lingers more than once on Ali, looking at his wife, as she gazes at the outside, and the female collective. In gazing at the peasant women, the sea, the mountain of Chenoua, the fields, Lila is liberating herself from the "Dakhil" [the inside] as well as from the male gaze. The film in its structuring of looks enacts a juxtaposition between the camera's looking at Ali, whose looking at Lila goes unnoticed, and Lila's looking at other women. Throughout the film, Lila makes her presence felt through her powerful self-gaze, and through the influence of her female, observational gaze—as when she looks at her female relatives of Chenoua or listens to their stories. The film captures in images the history of Lila's command of the gaze on others as well as on the outside. In *La Nouba* the spectator is also made to witness Lila's interaction with the Algerian women of her tribe in a realm which is under the control of the camera, but beyond the dominating control of patriarchal and colonial gazes.

Lila's self-gaze is crystallized in scenes where she addresses herself, in a poignant tone. In the first sequence of the film, the spectator is presented with an image of the protagonist, her face against the wall, repeating to herself statements that show her strong desire for silence and imprisonment: "Je parle, je parle, je parle. Je ne veux pas que tu me voie; je ne veux pas qu'il vienne me voir en vrai. Prisonnier. Le hasard m'a rendu prisonnier dans le silence et dans l'espace" [I speak, I speak, I speak. I don't want you to see me. I don't want him, indeed, to come to see me. Prisoner. chance has made me a prisoner within silence and space." Lila repeats three times "Je Parle," [I speak], which underlines the importance of oppositional female speech in the film. Prison, in her statement, is related to silence, as it is clear from the allusion to her female imprisonment. The wall against which she stands and the position in which she is standing with her back to the screen gives the viewer the impression that she is confined in a prison. Indeed, Lila is still imprisoned in the memories of a war that she cannot find a way to forget.

Djebar has admitted in her novel *Vaste est la prison* that Lila's words at the beginning of the film are hers (297). The film proceeds from an "I," which the spectator tends to associate with the filmmaker herself. The film, however, unfolds in such a way as to merge the autobiographical "I" with the voices of the women who made Algerian history. In the same scene in which Lila expresses her desire to speak, she also voices her longing for silence when she says: "J'avais quinze ans. J'avais cent ans de douleur. Je ne pouvais parler" [I was fifteen, but I had a hundred years of suffering. I could not speak]. Lila's moments of silence in the film, though, seem, to be volitional, contrary to the involuntary muteness of Ali following his accident. Her silence is also not to be understood as a result of the dominance of patriarchal speech or the male gaze, both of which are lacking in the film. The male, patriarchal gaze is subverted in the film through the absence of scenes showing requited gazing between Ali and

Lila. In different scenes that portray Ali gazing at Lila, the latter is either asleep or unaware of his gazes, undermining the influence of the male gaze in the film.

Male visual pleasure is also subverted in the film through the symbol of the veil. In the section of the film entitled "Btaihi," there is a scene comprised of whispering sounds and images of veiled women who are helping to bring weapons and ammunition down from the places where they were hidden in the mountain. Fanon has pointed out that the wearing of the veil by Algerian women was a symbol of active resistance against French colonialism; as he puts it in his "Algeria Unveiled":

> There is thus a historic dynamism of the veil that is very concretely perceptible in the development of colonization in Algeria. In the beginning, the veil was a mechanism of resistance, but its value for the social group remained very strong. The veil was worn because tradition demanded a rigid separation of the sexes, but also because the occupier was bent on unveiling Algeria. (63)

The hidden "looks" of the veiled women in the film resist the gaze of the French male who, in spite of his looking, is unable to see. The wearing of the veil was not a gender neutral resistance, for it also had a feminist resonance. The scene that portrays veiled women in the film stresses the ability of the veil to reject the gaze of the colonialist as well as the Algerian male, while allowing the veiled woman to assume the privilege of being the subject of the gaze, the one who looks without being seen. In his close analysis of the Algerian postcards which were sent by the French colonialists to France, Alloula remarks:

> The first thing the foreign eye catches about Algerian women is that they are concealed from sight...the eye cannot catch hold of her.... Draped in the veil that cloaks her to her ankles, the Algerian woman discourages the scopic desire (the voyeurism) of the photographer. She is the concrete negation of this desire and thus brings to the photographer confirmation of a triple rejection: the rejection of his desire, of the practice of his "art," and of his place in a milieu that is not his own. (7)

The veil indicates a negation of the "scopic drive" of the French male's gaze as well as of his presence in Algeria. Both Lila's self-gaze as well as the hidden looks of the veiled women highlight the subversive aspect of *La Nouba* in its double emphasis on Algerian women's physical visibility and the discursive power it signifies, as well as their veiling with its rejection of the patriarchal and the colonial gaze.

Female Space

La Nouba's female-centered images make it unique in Algerian cinematographic and cultural production, which has been marked until recently by the absence of images of Algerian women. It is in this figure of the Algerian woman that La Nouba's interventions in Algerian cinematographic productions lie. The female gaze in the film trespasses the spacial boundaries of Algerian society. Through the power of the female gaze, La Nouba explores female space, a space not previously represented in Algerian cinema. In doing so, La Nouba resonates with Moroccan female director Farida Benlyazid's film Bab Sma Maftouh [A Door to the Sky] (1988), which deploys female space in the context of liberally interpreted Islam. After her return from France to Fès to attend her father's funeral, Nadia, the protagonist, experiences a new sense of her self and her religion under the influence of Karina, an old religious woman. Nadia eventually decides to leave her French boyfriend and to turn the family mansion, which she inherited from her father, into a Zawiya for poor women and battered wives out of "Khayriya" [charity]. But while the film celebrates the Moroccan, Muslim female collective, it is similar to La Nouba in that it also expresses a double critique of both Islamic patriarchy as well as Orientalism.

In his critical reading of La Nouba, Réda Bensmaia has gone so far as to characterize La Nouba as a topography of female space. To understand La Nouba, he says, is to be able to relate to:

> ...the different places where women have lived for all time and invested their presence, places that traditional cinema had never been able to reconnoiter. In this sense, La Nouba presents not just a simple "(hi)story" of "feminine space," but, one might say, the lay of the land, its topography. It is a matter, above all, of making a topography of feminine places, the map of a continent as yet undiscovered, at the same time as inventing a new chronotope: that of feminine time(s). And this is what makes it possible to understand the mode of construction and the rhythm, or better yet the tempo and cadences, of Djebar's film. (Bensmaia 878)

Djebar, we might add, is presenting the Algerian woman in this film not as a category, but as an embodiment of female subjectivity. She extends the spectacle of the Algerian woman as image, which figures in earlier films, to her image as female space, which is occupied by Lila, as well as by the peasant women.

Lila has an important function in the film, since she is the one who presents the female image; she embodies the alternative Algerian female subjectivity, through which she expresses her refusal to abide by the gendered expectations that Algerian society imposes on women. It is this female dimension which probably accounts for the absence of any plot or action in the film. Mary Anne Doane has significantly noted how the figure of the woman in film is often associated with spectacle, space, or the image, in contrast with the linear flow of the plot: "With respect to a narrativization of the woman, the apparatus strains; but the transformation of the woman into spectacle is easy. Through her forced affinity with the iconic, imagistic aspects of cinema, the woman is constituted as a resistance or impedance to narrativization" (*Contemporary Film Theory* 167). Doane is referring here to Laura Mulvey's article, which I mentioned earlier, and especially to her argument that women are fetishized by the patriarchal structure of mainstream cinema, being turned into a spectacle to be looked at, to reassure the male spectator who would otherwise see women as symbolic of castration. The narrative of films stops at such moments, as we get close-ups of women's bodies on display, or long exhibitionist musical numbers that do not advance the plot. Femininity, both Doane and Mulvey argue, is not inherently anti-narrative, but it is patriarchy which constructs it as such. Within Hollywood cinema, the spectacle of the female figure is set against the narrative. What seems to account for the absence of plot or narrativization in *La Nouba*, however, is not patriarchal structure, in the way Mulvey points to Hollywood cinema, but rather the privileging of space over action in the film.

In his essay "Towards a Critical Theory of Third World Films," Teshome Gabriel argues that Third World cinema emphasizes the integrity of space in itself, whereas Western cinema portrays space only as the setting of action. The history of colonialism and the various forms of oppression in the neocolonial era provide the context of these Third World forms of film practice (Jim Pines and Paul Willem 44). While Gabriel's argument that all Third World people experience space and time differently from others reveals a certain essentialist and culturalist way of thinking on his part, *La Nouba* happens to endorse his argument that Third World film emphasizes space over action. *La Nouba* privileges the protagonist's constant drifting between places, as well as her journeys and quests, over any central action or plot. The camera often lingers for several seconds on the mountain and the plain fields of Chenoua. It was in open spaces that Lila was able to gaze into a female historical past.

The privileging of space in this film becomes understandable if we take into account the difficulty of action for Algerian women in the patriarchal and colonized Algeria. But contrary to Gabriel's assertion about the integrity of space in Third World cinema, *La Nouba* emphasizes rather the disintegrity of space in Algerian society. While space in *Bab Sma Maftouh* [Door to the Sky] is represented as female and Muslim, *La Nouba* suggests that space is variegated and complex. In one of the shots of the film, Lila, her husband and their daughter are shown visiting a Christian monument in the region of Chenoua. This scene only testifies to Djebar's view that space is heterogeneous in Algeria.

The combination of sounds and images highlights the complexity and the heterogeneity of women's experience of space in the film. The gendered space in the film is also connected with orality, which is peasant and not just feminine. The Algerian women imaged in the film occupy liberatory physical as well as psychological spaces. While the film shows images of veiled women, it also abounds in women's sounds: cries, screams, whispers, songs and chants. Such psychological female spaces are also enhanced by images of women involved in collective tasks that take place in physical, open spaces, such as harvesting, drawing water, fruit picking, etc.

Language

Lila's voice-over in *La Nouba* was first written in French, then translated into Arabic, and then rendered again in French in the French version.[9] By moving from French to Arabic and then back to French, the film enacts a dichotomization between the French voice-over narrator and the Algerian women who speak in the Arabic dialect in the film. The narrator's French voice-over which covers over the Algerian women's Arabic speech (which is in turn translated in French subtitles), forces us to ask whether translation is possible within the act of representation. The fact that the Algerian woman's Arabic speech is sometimes mistranslated and interrupted by French subtitles makes us also wonder about the loss involved in translation. The Arabic woman who speaks in the film cannot speak French; even if she could, a foreign language could never adequately represent the experience of the Algerian woman. In her essay "Diasporas Old and New: Women in the Transnational World," Gayatri Spivak has commented on the problematic task of the postcolonial translator when she says:

> Diaspora entails this task and permits its negligent performance. For diasporas also entail, at once, a necessary loss of contact with the idiomatic indispensability of the mother tongue. In the unexamined culturalism of academic diasporism, which ignores the urgency of transnationality, there is no one to check uncaring translations that transcode in the interest of dominant, feminist knowledge. (259-260)

According to Spivak, the translations of the postcolonial feminist intellectual mark the limits of her representation, for it is impossible for the foreign language to represent the true experience of the subaltern. Lila's hesitant act of listening, her French-over, and French subtitles in the film all exemplify the ways in which Djebar marks the limits of representation, and the way in which discourse determines how we hear and how we read the subaltern's speech.

While bad translation has often been seen as a limiting task which is conducive to misinterpretation, good translation can be enabling and useful for the postcolonial feminist intellectual in her cultural production. In order to understand Djebar's view of translation, we need first to examine the implications of bilingualism for her, as a Maghrebian intellectual. It is her film, Djebar claims, which has brought her back to writing, mainly because it has made her accept her linguistic bilingualism. She encapsulates her attitude towards her bilingualism in the following way: "Ce film m'a fait accepter mon bilinguisme culturel avec serenité. Mon rapport avec la langue Française est aujourd'hui plus clair. Si j'ecris en Français, c'est parce que j'ai choisi cette langue et non parce que je suis colonisée. De plus, pour me confronter avec la langue Arabe, je fais des traductions tous les deux ans" [This film has made me accept my bilingualism with serenity. If I write in French, it is because I have chosen this language, and not because I am colonized. My rapport with the French language is now clearer to me. Besides, in order to confront the Arabic language, I have been doing translations for the last two years] (*Jeune Afrique* 69). Confronting the Arabic language, according to Djebar, necessitates translation.

The nature of Djebar's relationship to Arabic brings to mind Abdelkebir Khatibi's philosophical thoughts on speech and language. For both of these francophone intellectuals, the process of decolonization requires drawing attention to the question of language.[10] For Khatibi, the task of the Maghrebian intellectual lies in bridging the gap between Arabic speech and other languages for "...translation requires a plurality of languages and of thoughts inscribed in them. And a "thought of difference," is a thought in languages, a universal translating of codes, of systems and of constellations of signs which circulate in the world and above it" (Khatibi 17-18). Djebar's relationship to her mother tongue is equally subversive, for she deploys translation to make the Arabic language express itself in a different language. By looking at the two different kinds of speech (French speech as well as Arabic speech) "contrapuntally," as constituting "intertwined and overlapping histories," the filmmaker seems also to be propounding a new political vision, one that Edward Said has called "...a post-imperial intellectual attitude [that] might expand the overlapping community between metropolitan and formerly colonized societies" (*Culture and Imperialism* 18). Translations in *La Nouba* mistranslate and interrupt the Algerian woman's speech not only to subvert, but also to create "difference" within the space or gap between the original Arabic speech and the French subtitles

Algerian (Female) History

The uniqueness of *La Nouba* stems also from its temporal dimensions which emphasize the importance of history and memory. In *Orientalism*, Said has drawn upon Anwar Abdel Malek's argument that Orientalism has considered the Oriental as an object of study endowed with a non-historical subjectivity (97). Said has elaborated further on this argument by insisting upon revisionist historiography and a re-reading of Orientalist discourse within the histories of the Oriental. Just as woman is constructed in patriarchal film as an image or spectacle which resists narrative, so does orientalism construct the colonized as a frozen image of otherness without history. Fanon has also drawn attention to the direct and indirect effects of colonialism on the colonized's past; as he puts it: "Colonialism is not satisfied merely with holding a people in its grip and emptying the native's head of all form and content. By a kind of perverted logic, it turns the past of the oppressed people, and distorts, disfigures and destroys it (*Wretched of the Earth* 161). Both Said and Fanon, though, fail to draw attention to the historical omissions of female historical agency from discourses of nationalism itself.

In order to understand the political implications of *La Nouba*, it is important to take into account the political and historical context in which it is situated. The film makes constant references to the anti-colonial resistance both in the nineteenth and twentieth centuries against the French conquest. In 1962, France recognized Algeria's independence, but the Algerian struggle continued, with the military's dictatorial rule in the name of nationalism and patriarchy. In 1976, a new Constitution and National charter passed that underscored the positive role played by women during the revolution and the need for their social emancipation.[11] In 1990, the FIS won more than five million votes, which brought the Islamists onto the political scene in Algeria. *La Nouba* was filmed in 1978, and thus makes no allusions to the violence in today's Algeria: the mass massacres of civilians, the violation of human rights, as well as the decapitations and throat slicing of intellectuals and journalists.

La Nouba, which was filmed fifteen years after Algeria won its independence, and before today's violent transgressions in Algeria, responds to both nationalism and patriarchy with a double critique. Djebar's project is to remind the Algerian public of women's positive role during Algeria's recent colonial history, and to recast the revolutionary subject as female. Images in this film do more fully express Algerian women's alternate, oppositional history, and make more explicit their participation and role in the Algerian nation. The project of locating Algerian women as subjects of an Algerian traditional culture, as well as of a national struggle, requires subverting colonial history in order to highlight the violence against women during French colonization. Although the history of Algerian resistance exists in documented form, as well as in the popular imagination, it is a predominantly male history, which is not inclusive of the "voices" of Algerian women. In his essay "Third Cinema as Guardian of Popular Memory: Towards a Third Aesthetics," Teshome Gabriel points to the "contradictions between official history and collective memory" (Jim Pines and Paul Willeman 56). It is around this idea of popular memory that *La Nouba* would qualify, according to Gabriel, as one of the many attempts in Third cinema in which "what is repressed in official versions of history is kept alive through collective accounts" (56).

As an historian, Djebar felt it necessary to have documentary evidence of Algerian women's history. Robert A. Rosenstone has pointed to the importance of oral history, interviews and images as evidence in film. He notes that history on film "is not history in the sense that academics think of it. It is history with different rules of representation, analysis and modes of reading and comprehension that we do not yet fully understand" (Rosenstone 1176). History as represented in film operates differently from academic history, for the rules normally expected from historical narrative such as straight chronology are often manipulated by the filmmaker, and devices such as flashbacks and flashforwards often interfere with the clear progression of the narrative. In addition to reproducing the stories as told her by Algerian women, the filmmaker has reorganized that historical evidence. *La Nouba* makes use of flashbacks to record historical events in Algerian women's anti-colonial struggle. Algerian women's war experiences in the film are at times enacted as nightmares which haunt Lila in her dreams. Lila's dream in the last movement of the film, titled "Khlas," for instance, reenacts Algerian women's resistance in random images and sounds of women in war. Oral history is also made evident in the film through repreated images of old women storytellers who are surrounded by children. Lila's voice-over comments on these scenes in the following manner: "Ainsi va l'Algerie muette. Toutes les vieilles, chaque nuit , chuchottaient, et l'histoire contée se repète..." [Thus goes the muted Algeria. All old women, every night, murmured, and the recounted past repeats itself...].

Djebar also deploys the medium of cinematic narration to relate the stories of Algerian heroines. The story of Zouleikha comes across in one of the sequences narrated by Lila's French voice-over. We are told that Zouleikha was born in the village of Hatchouk. She was married in 1945 to Oudai, an illiterate nationalist who was very politically active in the city of Cherchell. After November 1957, Hadj Oudai organized clandestine resistance, but he was later executed and his followers arrested. Zouleikha had decided to join the maquis at the age of forty. The French ultimately arrested her in the forest amidst the sounds of jeeps and police cars. To the crowd of partisans, who witnessed her arrest, Zouleikha screamed: "Why are you crying? See, all this turmoil is because of a woman." Lila's voice-over carries on with the story of Zouleikha in the following manner: "On parlera de la mort de Zouleikha, et de mes anciens jours de prison. Pour en parler, il faudra en être vraiment sortie, les tirer hors de ma mémoire" [I will speak of the death of Zouleikha, and of my old days in prison. To be able to speak, I need to be really free—free of these events which haunt my memory]. Lila later learnt about Zouleikha's fate from another woman. When Zouleikha was mutilated, after being tortured, her body disappeared the following night. A man from the maquis carried it on his back, and buried it in the forest: "Tu vois, il y a bien des façons d'offrir un tombeau à une femme" [You see, there are different ways to offer a tomb to a woman]. Unlike Bhubaneswari in Spivak's story, Zouleikha, in her armed struggle against colonialism and her act of resistance, was able to *speak*, prior to her death, to the agents of colonialism and patriarchy.

What was the Liberation?

Djebar seems to call in *La Nouba* for a kind of liberation for the Algerian woman which goes beyond her national resistance against colonialism. In one sequence of the film, Lila's words "Ouvrir de nouvelles prisons," [The opening of new prisons] which are followed by images of veiled women, show that, for Djebar, Algerian women's struggle for emancipation has not yet ended.[12] Djebar's idea of liberation seems to engage Edward Said's concept of liberation as a way beyond nativism. Said has clearly drawn the distinction between independence, nationalism, autonomy, etc., on the one hand, and liberation, on the other hand, dismissing nationalism and nativism as false forms of resistance to imperialism (*Culture and Imperialism* 229). Said rejects nativism as an essentializing form of nationalism, when he asserts that:"...to accept nativism is to accept the consequences of imperialism, the racial, religious, and political divisions imposed by imperialism itself" (292). The message of Djebar's film is that the nationalist consciousness that initiated independence must be differentiated from liberation. Decolonization for Algerian intellectuals like Djebar involves more than political resistance; it necessitates the decolonization of the mind from ideologies of dominance such as patriarchy and imperialism.

La Nouba's implicit critique of the domineering ideologies of modern Algeria also summons forth the philosophy of the Moroccan writer Abdelkébir Khatibi, who has often equated the decolonization of thought to "the affirmation of difference and an absolute and free subversion of the mind" (Khatibi 9). Although both Francophone writers, Djebar and Khatibi are different in their backgrounds and academic training. Djebar is an historian, while Khatibi is a philosopher; still, their approach of "double criticism" is an outcome of the crisis of modernization, which has emerged in the form of double-alienation experienced by Arab intellectuals from both Western culture and their own social and cultural formations. In *La Nouba*, the presence of Lila, the French educated daughter of the tribe, as well as of other images of young westernized Algerian women on their way to school, repeatedly emphasizes the point that Westernization is the materiality of Algerian modernity. Throughout the film, the image of Lila is posited against images of peasant women, and images of veiled, old Algerian women are juxtaposed against images of their unveiled liberated daughters. The film in its images enacts the double-alienation which Khatibi referred to when he spoke of the "silent interval between colonization and decolonization" and when he asked the people of the Third World to "follow a third way: ....a subversion that is in a way double, by which, by claiming the power of speech and action, goes to work in the context of a difference that is uncompromising" (11).

La Nouba can be viewed as a double critique of both French colonialism (and its imperialist ideology) and postcolonial (patriarchal) Algeria. The Arabic song that ends the film reinscribes a pessimistic view of modern Algeria. It is a celebration of the Algerian women who died for the revolution, as well as a plea for the liberation of the Algerian woman of the present who is still oppressed in modern Algeria:

> O Queens of Chenoua
> Accept my greetings
> Your heart has been distraught
> from the sufferings of the past
> Every evening
> Every morning
> You who understands the symbols

My song speaks always of freedom
I intercede for all the martyrs
so that others would not be oppressed
The sick woman will recover from her woes
She will say "I am liberated"
To the confined women
We have justified the veil
But now
begins the day of freedom.

NOTES

1. For more information on this topic, see Pierre Jeancolas 156.

2. For a detailed discussion of censorship in French cinema, and of how the 'Empire writes back" in Francophone cinema, refer to Dina Sherzer.

3. Ella Shohat has argued in her essay "Post-Third-Worldist Culture: Gender, Nation, and the Cinema" that Third World films which were directed by men "...were not generally concerned with a feminist critique of nationalist discourse. It would be a mistake to idealize the sexual politics of anti-colonial Third Worldist films like the classic *Battle of Algiers*, for example" (191).

4. In 1969 after the publication of her collection of poems *Poémes pour l'Algérie heureuse*, and her play *Rouge l'aube*, Assia Djebar stopped writing novels for a decade. In 1978, she directed her first feature film, *La Nouba*, which won the grand prize, Le Prix de la Critique Internationale, at the Venice film festival in 1979. After *La Nouba*, Djebar directed her second film *La Zerda ou les Chants de l'oubli*, in 1982, which is a documentary about the official history of the Maghreb. The name Zerda refers to a folklore dance in the south of Algeria. For a detailed overview of Assia Djebar's literary and cinematic productions, refer to "Chronology (Assia Djebar)."

5. All the above translations are my own.

6. I am taking here into account Assia Djebar's comments on the feminist aspects of her film in her introduction to the English version of *La Nouba* at the annual African Literature Association in East Lansing, Michigan, 1997.

7. Ella Shohat has used this phrase in her essay "Post-Third-Worldist Culture: Gender, Nation, and the Cinema" (183).

8. For a detailed definition of such cinematic concepts as "enunciation," "scopic drive" and "gaze," refer to Robert Stam, Robert Burgoyne and Sandy Flitterman-Lewis.

9. I am indebted for this information to Assia Djebar in her comments on *La Nouba* at the ALA., East Lansing, Michigan, 1997. In my reading of this

film, I am using the French version. Djebar introduced an English version of *La Nouba*, which will be available soon, at the same conference on April 18th, 1997.

10. For a detailed discussion of the nature of the francophone writer's relationship to the French language, refer to Albert Memmi.

11. For an overview of the historical events of Algeria, refer to Benjamin Stora. Nancy Woods has put together an unpublished chronology of events as summarized from Benjamin Stora's books.

12. In his meditation on the current social crisis in Algeria, Benamar Mediene wonders why the word "independence" substituted for the word "liberation" in 1962; as he put it: "Thus the word 'liberation' has only had a virtual existence, anticipating and mobilizing but disappearing once liberation was juridically achieved" (2). Benamar implies that after independence was won, the Algerian state has robbed Algerian people of their liberation.

WORKS CITED

Alloula, Malek. *The Colonial Harem*. Trans. Myrna Godzich and Wlad Godzich. Intro. Barbara Harlow. Minneapolis: University of Minnesota Press, 1986.

Bensmaia, Réda. "La Nouba des Femmes du Mont Chenoua: Introduction to the Cinematic Fragment." *World Literature Today* 70(4), Autumn 1996.

Fanon, Frantz. *A Dying Colonialism*. Chevalier, Haakon, tr. New York: Grove Weidenfeld, 1965.

______ *The Wretched of the Earth*. Trans. Farrington, Constance. New York: Grove Press, 1968.

Djebar, Assia. *La Nouba des Femmes du Mont Chenoua*. 1978.

______.*Zerda ou les Chants de l'oubli*. 1982

______.*Vaste est Le Prison*. Paris: Albin Michel, 1995.

______ *Women of Algiers in their Apartment*. Trans. Marjolijn de Jager. London: University Press of Virginia, 1980.

______."Interview" (with Oussila Tamzali) in *Cinéma Arabe*, 10-11.

Doane, Mary Anne. *Femmes Fatales: Feminism, Film Theory, Psychoanalysis*. NewYork: Routledge, 1991.

Jeancolas, Pierre. *Le Cinéma des Français; La Véme République* 1958-1978, Paris: Stock, 1979.

Khatibi, Abdelkébir. "Double Criticism: The Decolonization of Arab Sociology," in Barakat, Halim, ed. *Contemporary North Africa: Issues of Development and Integration*. Washington, D.C.: Center for Contemporary Arab Studies, 1985.

Mémmi, Albert. *The Colonizer and the Colonized.* Boston: Beacon Press, 1991(1965).

Mediene, Benamar. "Algeria: Social Crisis or Crisis of Meanings." Translated by Abdel Gaffeur This paper was delivered at a conference on Algeria at Cornell University on October 3rd, 1996.

Mulvey, Laura. *Visual and Other Pleasures.* Bloomington and Indianapolis: Indiana University Press, 1989.

Pines, Jim & Willem, P. ed. *Questions of Third Cinema.* London: BF1 Pub., 1989.

Rosenstone, Robert. "History in Images/History in Words: Reflections on the Possibility of Really Putting History onto Film," in *American Historical Review*, December 1988, *93*(5).

Said, Edward. *Orientalism.* NewYork: Vintage Books, 1978.

__________. *Culture and Imperialism.* NewYork: Knopt, 1993.

Sherzer, Dina, ed. *Cinema, Colonialism, Postcolonialism: Perspectives from the French and Francophone Worlds.* University of Texas Press: Austin, 1996.

Shohat, Ella. "Post-Third-Worldist Culture: Gender, Nation, and the Cinema," in Alexander, M. Jacqui and Mohanty, Chandra, eds. *Feminist Genealogies, Colonial Legacies, Democratic Futures.* Routledge: NewYork and London, 1997.

Smaoui Barrada. "Assia Djebar: Comment travaillent les écrivains," in *Jeune Afrique*, 27 June 1984.

Sora, Benjamin. *Histoire de L'Algérie Coloniale: 1830-1954*, 1994.

__________. *Histoire de La Guerre d'Algérie: 1954-1962*, 1993

Stam, Robert (etal). Eds. *New Vocabularies in Film Semiotics.* London & NewYork: Routledge, 1992.

Spivak, Gayatri. "Diasporas Old and New: Women in the Transnational World" This essay is the text of a paper delivered at Rutgers University in March, 1994.

__________. "Can the Subaltern Speak?" in Nelson, C & Grosserg, L., eds. *Marxism and the Interpretation of Culture.* Urbana: U of Illinois, 1988.

Winant, Winant. "Gayatri Spivak on the Politics of the Postcolonial Subject"(Interview), in *Socialist Review*, *90*(3), 1990.

7

A MAN IS BEING RAPED:
Nouri Bouzid's
Man of Ashes
and the Deconstruction of
Sexual Allegories of Colonialism

by Jarrod Hayes

Nouri Bouzid's *Rih Essed* [Man of Ashes] (1986), one of the first Tunisian films to reach a popular audience in Tunisia, opens on preparations for the marriage of Hachemi, its protagonist. Increasingly, however, the family romance on which Hachemi is about to embark is disrupted by images of the past, the haunting memories of a childhood rape that occurred when he was an apprentice woodworker. These images constitute a literal writing of the past, and the childhood memories they articulate are potential allegories of a more collective history.

It would be easy to perform a political, allegorical reading of the film in which Hachemi's rape becomes a figurative representation of the colonial penetration of North Africa *qua* symbolic rape. Although Hachemi is raped as a child by a Tunisian and not a foreigner, *Rih Essed* could easily fit into a tradition of Maghrebian national allegories in which the colonizer is represented by an indigenous collaborator. In Driss Chraïbi's *Le passé simple* (Morocco, 1954), for example, the protagonist's father, "Le Seigneur" or the Lord (against whom the protagonist revolts), has profited economically from French colonial rule even though he pretends to be a nationalist after Moroccan independence is virtually guaranteed. (He even introduces his son—the protagonist—to the future king of Morocco as a way of recuperating this filial revolt, an act that clearly allegorizes the recuperation of the national liberation movement by a neo-colonial ruling elite.) Likewise, in Rachid Boudjedra's *La répudiation* (Algeria, 1969), the target of the narrator's revolt—his father Si Zoubir, meaning Mr. Prick in the diminutive (Abdel-Jaouad 22Ð23) is friends with all the French judges in spite of his outwardly-appearing nationalist tendencies. Despite the fact that the revolts in both of these novels are against indigenous characters, they may be read as allegories of the national liberation movements against French colonial rule, whose authority is represented in the figure of the traditional authority of the father. In a reading of *Rih Essed* in which Hachemi's rape allegorizes the colonization of Tunisia, the master's authority over the apprentice (which, as will become clear below, has its own paternal characteristics) plays this role.

In addition, *Rih Essed* reinforces the association of rape and colonization with another sexual cliché of certain nationalist discourses, that of colonization as a form of prostitution. Here the association is much more literal as Hachemi's friends take him to a brothel for a sort of bachelors' party. The madam, Sejra (Arabic for tree), has tattooed on her chest the names of various notables from the colonial era and her halls are filled with the portraits of the Tunisian elite that collaborated with the French during the protectorate. Though prostitution has been used to allegorize colonization in a wide variety of anti-colonial discourses—from Frantz Fanon's description of the "unveiling" of Algeria to the more general description of Orientalist discourse and colonization of the Middle East by Edward W. Said—in Sejra's brothel, this allegorical deployment of prostitution acquires a Tunisian specificity, particularly in the role of the procuress. The images of the indigenous elites, with whom Sejra identifies so completely that she has their names permanently inscribed on her body, testify to the specific colonial form of the protectorate, which (unlike direct rule in Algeria) required the collaboration of the Tunisian elite. On an allegorical level, the intermediary role of the madam would represent the Tunisian elite that prostituted its own people to French colonial rule. Indeed, Sejra looks back on the colonial era with nostalgia, and not merely as the site of her lost youth. She also sees herself as having had considerably more power because of her influence on the powerful men who were her clients: "La règne de Sejra est revolue" [Sejra's rule is a thing of the past], she states, and, "Je ne commande plus rien" [I no longer command anything] (from the French subtitles). In short, she ruled, and Tunisia was prostituted. Thus, the brothel scene, as well as Hachemi's memories, may be read as an allegory of the history of Tunisia's colonization.

In "Third World Literature in the Era of Multinational Capitalism," Fredric Jameson writes, "Third-world texts, even those which are seemingly private and invested with a properly libidinal dynamic—necessarily project a political dimension in the form of national allegory:

*the story of the private individual destiny is always an allegory of the
embattled situation of the public third-world culture and society"* (69).
Aijaz Ahmad has articulated a thorough critique of Jameson's
generalization by challenging a number of its assumptions, the first of
which is that there is such a thing as the "Third World"—"we live not in
three worlds but one" ("Jameson" 103)—and therefore a "Third World
Literature": "[T]here is no such thing as a 'Third World Literature' which
can be constructed as an internally coherent object of theoretical
knowledge" (96–97). Ahmad also points out that Jameson's notion of
national allegory privileges the Nation in a way that contradicts his
discussion of multinational capitalism, which tends to de-emphasize
national boundaries. The "Three Worlds Theory," Ahmad argues, assumes
that capitalism is restricted to the "First World" and socialism to the
"Second." According to him, however, capitalism is global (and on this
point he agrees with Jameson) as is resistance to it, which he calls by the
name of socialism. In addition, Ahmad maintains that not all so-called
"Third World Literature" is necessarily allegorical and that "First World
Literature," particularly subaltern "First World Literature," often is. Yet by
asserting the possibility of allegorical readings of certain "First World"
literary texts, Ahmad at least tacitly acknowledges the possibility of
reading some works of what is often called "postcolonial literature" as
allegories.[1] Since Ahmad's desire is to deprivilege the national, he frames
his notion of allegory in terms of the distinction between public and
private: "If we replace the idea of the "nation" with that larger, less
restrictive idea of 'collectivity,' and if we start thinking of the process of
allegorization not in nationalistic terms but simply as a relationship
between private and public, personal and communal, then it also becomes
possible to see that allegorization is by no means specific to the so-called
Third World" (110).

In Maghrebian novels in French, allegory, whether one labels it as
national or otherwise, can be a helpful concept in understanding the textual
and sexual politics of certain novels. Kateb Yacine's *Nedjma* (1956), for
example, often read as *the* novel of Algerian identity, encourages such an
allegorical reading; the eponymous character's return to the ancestral
village represents a collective return to national origins or roots that will
allow the Algerian people to consolidate the national consciousness
necessary to oppose French colonial rule. Even an earlier style of
Maghrebian novels, which one might classify as childhood narratives, can
be read as allegories of a collective experience of colonization. Thus Albert
Memmi's *La statue de sel* (1953)—which tells the story of a Jewish
Tunisian's education in the French colonial school system, his attempt to
assimilate into French culture, and his resulting alienation—might be read

as an allegory of not only the alienation of an entire class of French-educated elite *evolués*, but also an alienation of a more directly economic sort, that is, the expropriation of Tunisian land and goods that was the mainstay of colonialism.[2]

Jameson's discussion suggests "a radically different and objective relationship of politics to libidinal dynamics" (80) and thus elaborates on *Marxism and Form* (1971), where his previous discussion of Walter Benjamin emphasizes the political potential of allegorical readings. According to Jameson, in Benjamin's work, "allegory is restored to us—not as a sign of the medieval health of the essentially religious spirit, but rather as a pathology with which in the modern world we are only too familiar" (72). In contrast with Medieval thinkers and their deployments of allegory, Benjamin "replac[ed] theology with politics" (61), so that allegory might become an important genre for Marxist criticism. In "Défendre la diversité culturelle au Maghreb," Tahar Ben Jelloun describes a similar relation between the sexual and the political in the Maghrebian novel's "audace dans la contestation de l'ordre sexuel et dans la transgression des tabous, surtout d'ordre sexuel" [audacity in contesting the social order and in the transgression of taboos, especially sexual ones], and he characterizes this audacity as a tentative de dévoilement, [une] porte ouverte sur un secret, sur un bien caché" (272) [an attempt to unveil, a door opening onto a secret, onto a hidden wealth]. I would argue that Maghrebian sexual allegories of the political constitute one arena in which sexual transgressions are deployed for their political force. In Boudjedra's *Les 1001 années de la nostalgie* (1979), for example, a village revolts against foreign filmmakers who come to film an Orientalist version of the *Arabian Nights*—a revolt that allegorizes the Algerian revolution as well as resistance to a post-independence indigenous elite (personified by the governor, Bender Chah, who collaborates with the foreigners). Here, gender insubordination plays a crucial role: the governor's wife defends herself against a would-be rapist among the filmmakers by cutting off his penis with a fan used to propel magic carpets in the film; a historical armed struggle carried out by the village women against the men serves as an inspiration for the current revolt; and the ongoing revolution threatens to invert traditional gender roles to such an extent that the village men begin to fear being forced into seclusion once a month to wait out their menstrual periods on chamber pots. Yet this political use of the sexual, as I attempt to demonstrate here, also has its problems. In contrast with Ahmad's critique of Jameson's notion of the "national allegory," a critique not of political allegory per se but of Jameson's inaccurate generalizations and his use of problematic political terms such as the "Third World" (whose dangerous assumptions Ahmad reveals in the terms' genealogies), this essays considers the sexual politics of the genre, which may be even more inherently problematic than Ahmad suggests.

Just as *Rih Essed* lends itself to a reading in which the sexual allegorizes the political, it also suggests that such allegories imply a dangerous sexual politics. In *Allegories of Reading* (1979), Paul de Man argues that "any narrative is primarily the allegory of its own reading, the narrative of its own deconstruction" (76–77). While his statement might not always be true, many of the Maghrebian national allegories mentioned above also involve a deconstruction of *official* nationalist discourse or *official* prescriptions of national identity. Likewise, Bouzid's film seems to deconstruct the national allegory it simultaneously proposes. For the family romance that the memory of rape disrupts is just as much an object of critique as the rape itself; thus, the film suggests, not all of the rape's effects are entirely negative. By blurring the distinction between past and present, and therefore that between Hachemi's adult masculinity (in the film's narrative present) and his not-yet masculine childhood, *Rih Essed* stages the failure of the sexual allegory of colonization, which would require the separateness of the past from the present in order to narrate memory as history.

Sexual Allegories of Colonialism

Sexual allegories have long been used by both pro- and anti-colonial commentators to describe the process of colonization. In a reading of French accounts of the colonial invasion of Algeria, Assia Djebar describes the invaders' comparison of conquest to a deflowering, a rape:

> Ce monde étranger, qu'ils pénétraient quasiment sur le mode sexuel, ce monde hurla continûment vingt ou vingt-cinq années durant, après la prise de la Ville Imprenable. Y pénètrent comme en une défloration. L'Afrique est prise malgré le refus qu'elle ne peut étouffer. (*L'Amour, la fantasia* 70)

> [This alien world, which they penetrated as they would a woman, this world sent up a cry that did not cease for two score years or more after the capture of the Impregnable City. Penetrated and deflowered; Africa is taken, in spite of the protesting cries that she cannot stifle. (*Fantasia* 57)]

In *Orientalism*, Edward W. Said gives sexual meaning not only to the physical penetration of colonial invasion, but also to the epistemological penetration involved in coming to *know* the Orient: "[T]he relation between the Middle East and the West is really defined as sexual. The Middle East is resistant, as any virgin would be, but the male scholar wins the prize by bursting open, penetrating through the Gordian knot despite 'the taxing task'" (309). Whereas in the above passage Said allegorizes

Orientalist discursive production (and by implication the colonization it parallels) as a deflowering, a rape, in his discussion of Flaubert, prostitution serves this allegorical purpose: "Flaubert's encounter with an Egyptian courtesan produced a widely influential model of the Oriental woman. [The] historical facts of domination allowed him not only to possess Kuchuk Hanem physically but to speak for her. Flaubert's situation of strength in relation to Kuchuk Hanem was not an isolated instance. It fairly stands for the pattern of relative strength between East and West, and the discourse about the Orient that it enabled" (6).

One finds a similar use of sexual images in some anti-colonial nationalist discourses. Marie-Aimée Helie-Lucas, for example uses rape to describe coerced unveilings of Algerian women:

> During the war, French officials had insisted that Algerian women should be freed from the oppression of the veil. French army trucks had transported village women to urban areas. There these women were forced to unveil publicly thereby proving their renunciation of outworn traditions. Both Algerian men and women resented this symbolic public rape. (108)

Likewise, in his essay "Algeria Unveiled" (originally published in 1959), Frantz Fanon uses unveiling as a metaphor for colonization and describes this "unveiling" as a rape: "Every veil that fell, every body that became liberated from the embrace of the traditional *haïk*, every face that offered itself to the bold and impatient glance of the occupier, was a negative expression of the fact that Algeria was beginning to deny herself and was accepting the rape of the colonizer" (42). In addition, he states that colonialist fantasies of raping Algerian women were often preceded by an unveiling: "Thus the rape of the Algerian woman in the dream of a European is always preceded by a rending of the veil. We witness here a double deflowering" (45). Through his metaphorical use of unveiling, Fanon, like Said, associates rape with prostitution as possible allegories of colonialism; for the unveiled Algerian "girl" is equated with an "easy" one, i.e., a prostitute: "An unveiled Algerian girl who 'walks the street' is very often noticed by young men who behave like young men all over the world, but who use a special approach as the result of the idea people habitually have of one who has discarded the veil. She is treated to unpleasant, obscene, humiliating remarks" (53).

Some feminist critics, however, have questioned the use of sexual metaphors in male nationalist discourses such as Fanon's. Winifred Woodhull, for example, points out that since "Algeria is personified as one woman" in "Algeria Unveiled" (3), Fanon's essay serves "to obscure tensions that have always existed between nationalism and feminism in Algeria" (22–23). One might also say that the national allegory, in which the unveiling of Algerian women represents the colonization and then decolonization of Algeria, effaces women's concerns by making those of the Nation their equivalents. In other words, in Fanon's treatment, women's concerns are relevant only insofar as they further the national struggle. I would suggest that other uses of the sexual in certain nationalist discourses carry a similar danger. If colonialism is a rape or a form of prostitution, the struggle for decolonization could easily become a matter of effacing this affront to the Nation's honor. When the rape of a woman allegorizes colonization, colonization constitutes an affront to male honor and to the colonized man's masculinity, which is embodied in the integrity of the Nation's women, as if the greatest victims when women are raped were men. The same holds true when prostitution serves the same allegorical purpose. Decolonization then becomes a matter of restoring a supposedly pre-colonial sexual purity, a restoration one might describe as an imposition of sexual normativity. These sexual allegories of the political, then, serve to occlude the literal violence done to women (or men), not only in rape (or prostitution) but also by colonialism, and contribute discursively to the continued marginalization of women and non-normative sexualities after independence and the replacement of the colonizer by a national elite.

In *The Wretched of the Earth* (1962), Fanon warned against the misuse of national consciousness that might allow a national elite to replace the colonizer after independence.[3] His prediction has come true in most African countries, and in Algeria, the very women Fanon described participating in the Algerian revolution are now the battleground for the struggle between the ruling elite and its armed fundamentalist opposition. While Fanon understood the dangers of nationalism, his relegation of issues of gender and sexuality to a secondary status in relation to the national struggle had political implications he clearly did not foresee. For the subordination of these issues to national ones has continued after independence and, as the Algerian case proves, actually contributes to the new ruling class's consolidation of power. Put bluntly, the sexual politics Fanon uncritically articulated actually contributed to the coming to power of the national elite he warned against.

Jameson's notion of the national allegory, in which the sexual is only of interest insofar as it represents the national, might thus be said to share Fanon's sexual politics, particularly when the sexual in question is assumed to be organized along normative lines. An allegorical reading of *Rih Essed*, for example, in which Hachemi's rape represents the colonization of Tunisia, would necessarily equate decolonization with Hachemi's marriage (which the rape endangers and whose successful conclusion would mean that the ghosts of the past have been laid to rest).

While the fate of Algerian women after independence has little in common with that of Tunisian women, and the Bourguiba regime's legalization of abortion and abolition of polygamy soon after independence represent gains for Tunisian women unavailable to other Maghrebian women (or indeed, in the case of abortion, to many Western women at the time), *Rih Essed* suggests that the dangers Fanon failed to see in the Algerian context should also be avoided in a Tunisian one.

A Man Is Being Raped

The most obvious way in which the film is at odds with the usual clichés of rape and prostitution as allegories of colonization is that it allegorizes colonialism with the rape of a man. It is important to emphasize the "rape of a man" because, in the context of the film, the violence of a child's violation has meaning only as it continues to do violence to an adult male whose masculinity is thereby questioned. This is not to dismiss the trauma experienced by Hachemi as a child, however "real" it must have been. The film simply does not deal with this trauma, but with that which Hachemi experiences as a man. This narrative of the memory of a violence that continues to do violence in the present is the potential allegory of colonial history, in which the negative effects of the past continue in the post-independence present. If these lingering effects of colonialism include neo-colonialism, then the return of repressed memories of the past could be said to be at work in indigenous personifications of both colonial and neo-colonial authority in other works of Maghrebian fiction (such as Bender Chah in *Les 1001 années de la nostalgie* and the fathers in *Le passé simple* and *La répudiation*).

But the return of this past has an effect that the film does not seem to entirely condemn: it interrupts the family romance Hachemi is about to undertake. When Hachemi announces that he does not want to get married, his father beats him with a belt in front of the entire family. Indeed, the structural position of the father in the film parallels that of Ameur, the master who raped him. In his discussion of the film, Aziz Krichen writes, "Dans l'univers des corporations artisanales, le maître initiateur est une seconde figure du père, c'est le principal substitut du père biologique" (19). [In the world of artisans' guilds, the initiating master is a second father figure; he is the main substitute of the biological father.] (Interestingly, as Ameur is dying, he proclaims, "Je vous ai pourtant initiés." [After all, I'm the one who initiated you.] This initiation was obviously sexual as well as professional.) The father, after all, confided his son to Ameur, and both father and master are portrayed as sources of violence. Yet the memory of the former violence challenges Hachemi's masculinity as well as the family structure policed and upheld by the father. In one scene, girls of the family affirm, "Hachemi est si blanc de peau, il aurait dû être une fille" [Hachemi has such white skin; he should have been a girl.] The film even seems to offer up Hachemi to the desiring gaze of the spectator, a fact a number of film critics have noticed. "Caméra de chair," a review of the film in the official Tunisian French-language newspaper *La presse*, states:

> Regardez comment Hachemi et Farfat sont filmés. Ils sont interrogés dans leur chair. La caméra est si proche de leur corps qu'on la dirait collée à leur peau. Nous voyons les corps, nous les regardons, nous les sentons. Nous nous sentons si proches des personnages que nous avons l'impression de les toucher, de les caresser presque, comme si par les douceurs de ses mouvements, la caméra cherchait à soigner les corps de leur blessure.

> [Notice how Hachemi and Farfat are filmed. Their very flesh is interrogated. The camera is so close to their bodies that it could be said to be glued to their skin. We see their bodies, we look at them, we feel them. We feel so close to the characters that we have the impression of touching them, almost caressing them, as if by the tenderness of its movements, the camera sought to heal the bodies of their wounds.][4]

Thus the memory of rape is not the only thing that feminizes Hachemi; the film reinforces the rape's feminizing effect by turning him into an object of desire for the male spectator, whose gaze, as Laura Mulvey has shown, constitutes its object as feminine.

Hachemi's childhood friend, Farfat, also raped by Ameur, experiences a similar difficulty in asserting his masculinity. Writing on the walls proclaims, "Farfat is not a man." Farfat's father has kicked him out of the house (possibly for this reason), and in the brothel scene, another childhood friend, Azaiez, attempts to caress him while dancing. Azaiez's repeated refusal to abide by Farfat's rejections of his advances leads to a fight after which Azaiez recalls aloud the childhood rape. After this (semi) public unveiling of the secrets of the past, Farfat goes out and kills Ameur, thereby washing his masculinity clean in his rapist's blood. The film ends by affirming Farfat's newly proven masculinity as a boy erases the writing on the walls after Farfat has successfully escaped the police.[5] Farfat, described throughout the film as the character who will never overcome his marginality, thus has an easier time proving his manhood than Hachemi, whose parallel opportunity to affirm his masculinity would occur on the wedding night, as his mother constantly reminds him, when the blood-stained sheet would presumably be displayed for all to see.

In a sense, Hachemi, like Farfat, must prove his masculinity with blood, that of his bride. The consummation of the marriage never happens, however, and it is unclear whether the film "intends" the spectator to assume the marriage will occur after the film ends. Instead, the wedding night is replaced with two imperfect imitations that preclude the conclusion of the family romance: Hachemi's masturbatory rehearsal of the wedding night in his new apartment, and the staging of a wedding consummation in the brothel scene, where a prostitute plays the role of Hachemi's newly wed. In both instances, however, the blood-stained sheets are missing, which sets the film's libidinal economy outside of the structures and framework of marriage and the family.

Memory and History

In the film, Hachemi is raped *as a man* not merely because the memory of a childhood rape continues to traumatize him, but also because the film deconstructs the division between past and present. Exactly what constitutes the past and what constitutes the "real" diegetic time of the film's narrative present become increasingly unclear. A conventional technique for representing the past or memory in film (or any narrative form for that matter) is the flashback. Technically, again in conventional terms, the flashback is framed in film through montage. In *Man of Ashes*, this would first involve a shot of the adult Hachemi. The film would then cut to a scene with Hachemi as a child (played by a younger actor)[6] and back to the film's narrative present—a device used several times in the film. In this scenario, the cut clearly marks the separation between past and present. In two instances of remembrance in the film, however, this distinction is not so clear cut.

In the first of these scenes there is no cut. Walking through the medina of Sfax, the adult Hachemi looks at a younger boy (perhaps his younger self), and both are represented in the same frame. The woman standing in a doorway who invites the adult Hachemi to approach (maybe because she is a prostitute) is the same one who comforts him after his rape as a child, which is visualized on screen after the adult Hachemi sees her. She is perhaps merely a hallucination in the film's narrative present, but at any rate, the presence of the same character (with no age difference) in both the film's past and present signals a blurring between the two. Thus, temporally, in this scene at least, there seems to be no difference between child and adult Hachemis. The image that perhaps best describes this infection of the present by the past is that of a haunting, in which the dead literally comes back to life.

One witnesses a haunting in the second scene when Hachemi returns to his own workshop at night. Burdened by childhood memories, he sits in a rocking chair, and a door closes by itself (as if done by a ghost). Another door closes; at first it seems to close by itself, but as it turns out, it is closed by the rapist. The rape scene is then visualized. Here, the memory of rape is so powerful that it can close doors in the film's narrative present. These flashbacks/memories haunt the present in a very real sense. Hachemi does not merely go back to his childhood memories; rather, remembering brings them back. The fact that two shots of doors closing are used to frame the cut that marks a flashback is, I would suggest, not innocent. The association of doors with memories—even in the first scene, one hears the sound of closing doors as Hachemi walks through the medina, and the woman (coded as a prostitute) is half hidden behind a door—serves to emphasize the haunting that occurs when memories appear from behind closed doors, i.e., the doors that were closed to permit the occurrence of a rape. In a sense, one could say that the doors that close off the rape scene from public view create a sort of closet. I say public view and not public discourse because both Farfat and Hachemi's rapes circulate in public discourse as an "open secret" that other men can use as a trump card whenever they need to take advantage of what Eve Kosofsky Sedgwick has called the blackmailability of masculinity (84).[7] Thus, in addition to the skeletons of the past hidden in the closet, Hachemi encounters behind closed doors the secrets of masculinity, that which constantly lies waiting, the continual threat of emasculation. One might even say that masculinity is always haunted in this way since the threat of its loss (castration) is what drives its constant reproduction in acts such as the murder in the film. The fact that masculinity is haunted from within as well as from without is emphasized in the film when we learn that it was Farfat who wrote the graffiti that questions his own manhood.

The family romance Hachemi is supposed to begin writing for himself is also haunted in *Rih Essed*. In this case, the figure of the prostitute plays the role of specter. It is no coincidence that the final and most vivid flashback recalling the rape occurs in the brothel and that, in the first flashback described above, a prostitute comforts the young Hachemi as she almost simultaneously beckons the adult Hachemi. As the film situates the father in a parallel position to the rapist's, in the flashback, the film cuts to Hachemi's mother comforting him with the exact same gestures of the prostitute, thereby comparing mother to prostitute. In the brothel scene as well, Sejra admits to wanting a son, and Hachemi wishes to withdraw into the brothel forever and, therefore, to turn it into his home, which would imply transforming Sejra into his mother. If prostitution and rape are allegories of colonization, what is one to make of marriage and the family, which the film seems to associate with both rape and prostitution? Again, the very marriage that would reconcile Hachemi with a previous violence (and, on an allegorical level, represent Tunisia's reconciliation with a colonial past through decolonization) is implicated in the same violence. Likewise, when Hachemi unveils the prostitute dressed as a Western-style bride in the brothel performance of the wedding night, the film not only recalls the Fanonian association, discussed above, of unveiling and prostitution, but also associates marriage with prostitution.[8] In case the Western spectator might tend to restrict the marriage/prostitution comparison to Maghrebian, Arab, or Muslim marriages, the "unveiling" that traditionally occurs in even contemporary American marriages is also implicated in the film's critique of the family romance.

The "unveiling" of the prostitute/bride in the brothel scene, however, is not the only unveiling that occurs in the film. When the fight breaks out between Farfat and Azaiez, Sejra accuses them of bringing their dirty laundry to wash in her brothel. *Rih Essed* itself also unveils the secrets that should remain in the closet of Hachemi's past and displays his dirty laundry for all spectators to see. The film unveils Hachemi as if he were the prostitute and, therefore, could also be said to prostitute him not only to Ameur, but also to the film's spectators. The unveiling performed by the film thus fits as much into Ben Jelloun's paradigm of unveiling sexual secrets as into Fanon's paradigm of unveiling as a sign of accepting the colonizer's symbolic rape. As in Ben Jelloun's notion of unveiling, linked as it is to a post-independence resistance to the status quo, in *Rih Essed*, unveiling secrets from the past, along with the deconstruction of the past/present distinction and of masculinity, has political implications for an allegorical reading of the film. If the memories of a childhood rape constantly haunt the adult Hachemi, Tunisia, at the allegorical level, would still be haunted by a colonial past, by the history (allegorized by memory) of colonial rape, of the colonial prostitution of Tunisia.

It is here that we are confronted with the limits of this particular allegorical reading as well as its dangers. If the colonial past is also part of the present, if there is no returning to a pre-colonial past, what would it mean to attempt to cleanse the Nation's honor of the affront represented by this symbolic rape? The political desire to return to a mythic past or purity also conceals its own dangers. Witness again the fundamentalist opposition in Algeria, which claims the project of returning Algeria to such a past. Like the regime in power, this opposition also turns women into an *enjeu* as both veiled and unveiled women are caught in the crossfire between warring factions. The Algerian example clearly demonstrates the danger of returning to such a pre-colonial past for women. *Rih Essed* also seems to suggest that the reconciliation with the past allegorized by traditional or normative family structures implies a similar danger. In sexual allegories of the political, when the allegorical sexuality continues to reproduce sexual and patriarchal hierarchies, the hierarchies risk being reproduced at the political or national level. Thus, Fanon's allegorical unveiling/rape/prostitution has paradoxically led to a literal reveiling of women in present-day Algeria, and in the film, the cleansing of masculinity can only occur through the spilling of blood. In the case of the bride's blood, which would be displayed after the marriage's consummation, effacing the affront to masculinity represented by Hachemi's rape would require another deflowering, this one perpetrated by the victim of the previous one. As long as questions of decolonization require the enforcement of masculinity, women and un-masculine men (like Hachemi) will suffer the consequences. The danger of making sexuality a scapegoat in the struggle for decolonization is that dealing with the past violence of colonization may require sacrificing new victims to another kind of violence.

Since an allegorical reading implies that the literal story parallels another narrative at a *higher* level, to a certain extent, Jameson's national allegory may establish the separateness of the sexual and political levels (with the former subordinated to the latter) even as it argues for their connectedness; Jameson's notion of a sexual allegory of the political risks leaving unquestioned the sexual/political dichotomy which assumes that the personal is *not* political to begin with. Since the film uses memories of a sexual past to allegorize and deallegorize a supposedly more political history, the past/present dichotomy becomes implicated in that between sexuality and politics. Because a man's past is his childhood, i.e., when he was not (yet) a man, the deconstruction of the present/past dichotomy through the film's erosion of the conventional flashback is also the deconstruction of masculinity. The film also demonstrates that the threat to masculinity (in Hachemi's case) comes not only from the past but is also ever present as that absence (lack) that Man seeks to avoid by asserting his masculinity. Whereas condoning the rape of a boy or the symbolic rape of colonization is out of the question, the film actively participates in the deconstruction of Hachemi's masculinity, one of the implications of the childhood rape. *Rih Essed* thus seems to propose a non-masculinist model of decolonization that cherishes rather than opposes affronts to masculinity. The current Algerian situation as a successor to the masculinist nationalist ideal represented by Fanon's allegory of colonial rape and prostitution makes it clear that Tunisia is not Algeria; *Rih Essed* seems to carefully guard this difference and hope to maintain it.

I would like to thank Fazia Aïtel, Maureen Eke, Frieda Ekotto, Kenneth W. Harrow, Carina Yervasi, and Emmanuel Yewah for reading this essay and for their valuable suggestions. I would especially like to thank Maher Ben Moussa for his thorough reading and extensive comments, and for helping me to verify the accuracy of the French translations in the subtitles of certain Arabic dialogues.

NOTES

1. Ahmad has also criticized the term "postcolonial" (see "The Politics of Literary Postcoloniality").

2. On reading the childhood narratives as national allegories, see my "Rachid O. and the Return of the Homopast: The Autobiographical as Allegory in Childhood Narratives by Maghrebian Men."

3. I should point out that while Fanon spoke of a national bourgeoisie's stepping into the colonizer's shoes, he did not suggest the two were exactly the same. The national bourgeoisie, for Fanon, is not a bourgeoisie in the true sense, since it lacks the necessary capital to be so. It also lacks the power and experience (at least in the period directly following independence) to maintain its authority in the more subtle ways of its European and American counterparts, hence the recourse to such methods as military dictatorship, fascism, one-party rule, and kleptocracy.

4. The review is simply signed T.C. and is included in the press packet sold with the video by La Médiathèque des Trois Mondes (which does not give the page numbers in the original). Likewise, Elliott Stein writes, "Bouzid's camera has photographed the striking Imed Maalal (Hachemi) with as much tender loving care as Von Sternberg's lenses ever devoted to Marlene" (95). Mark Halleck writes, "Imed Maalal, who plays Hachemi, is gorgeous; the camera drools over him, pawing at his cheek bones in close-up, fixating on the seat of his pants in medium long shots as he endlessly walks the streets" (32).

5. One could extend the allegorical reading to the role of the police representatives of the post-independence state—who are thus on the side of the rapist in a Fanonian association of the post-independence elite and the former colonizer.

6. In earlier Hollywood films, this scene might also be set apart with soft focus or a variety of other similar techniques.

7. Sedgwick also uses the term "open secret" to describe the closet (67).

8. Paradoxically, the only women the film represents as being in any way veiled are prostitutes. With the exception of the prostitute who comforts Hachemi in the first flashback described above, all wear the *sefsari*, a Tunisian outer garment that can, if needed, be pulled over the head and part of the face. (Sejra wears one without covering her head.) (Many thanks to Maher Ben Moussa for explaining this garment and its distinction from the veil proper.)

WORKS CITED

Abdel-Jaouad, Hédi. "'Too much in the sun': Sons, Mothers, and Impossible Alliances in Francophone Maghrebian Writing." *Research in African Literatures* 27.3 (1996): 15–33.

Ahmad, Aijaz. "Jameson's Rhetoric of Otherness and the 'National Allegory.'" In *Theory: Classes, Nations, Literatures*. London: Verso, 1992. 95–122.

———. "The Politics of Literary Postcoloniality." *Race and Class* 36.3 (1995): 1–20.

Ben Jelloun, Tahar. "Défendre la diversité culturelle au Maghreb. *L'état du Maghreb*. Ed. Camille and Yves Lacoste. Paris: La Découverte, 1991. 271 72.

Boudjedra, Rachid. *Les 1001 années de la nostalgie*. Paris: Deno'l, 1979.

———. *La répudiation*. Paris: Deno'l, 1969.

Chraïbi, Driss. *Le passé simple*. Paris: Denoël, 1954.

de Man, Paul. *Allegories of Reading: Figural Language in Rousseau, Nietzsche, Rilke, and Proust*. New Haven: Yale UP, 1979.

Djebar, Assia. *L'amour, la fantasia*. Paris: Lattès, 1985.

———. *Fantasia, an Algerian Calvacade*. Trans. Dorothy S. Blair. Portsmouth, NH: Heinemann, 1993.

Fanon, Frantz. *Les damnés de la terre*. Paris: Maspero, 1962.

———. "Algeria Unveiled." *A Dying Colonialism*. Trans. Haakon Chevalier. New York: Grove, 1965. 35–67.

———. *Sociologie d'une révolution: L'an V de la révolution algérienne*. Paris: Maspero, 1959.

———. *The Wretched of the Earth*. Trans. Constance Farrington. New York: Grove, 1963.

Halleck, Mark. Review of *Rih Essed*. *The New York Native* 26 Jan. 1987: 23.

Hayes, Jarrod. "Rachid O. and the Return of the Homopast: The Autobiographical as Allegory in Childhood Narratives by Maghrebian Men." *Sites* 1.2 (1997). Forthcoming.

Helie-Lucas, Marie-Aimée. "Women, Nationalism and Religion in the Algerian Liberation Struggle." *Opening the Gates: A Century of Arab Feminist Writing*. Ed. Margot Badran and Miriam Cooke. Bloomington: Indiana UP, 1990. 105–14.

Jameson, Fredric. *Marxism and Form: Twentieth-Century Dialectical Theories of Literature*. Princeton: Princeton UP, 1971.

______. "Third World Literature in an Age of Multinational Capitalism. *Social Text* 15 (1987): 65–88.

Kateb, Yacine. *Nedjma*. Paris: Seuil, 1956.

Krichen, Aziz. *Le syndrome Bourguiba*. Tunis: Cérès, 1993.

Memmi, Albert. *La statue de sel*. 1953. Paris: Gallimard, 1966.

Mulvey, Laura. "Visual Pleasure and Narrative Cinema." *Visual and Other Pleasures*. Bloomington: Indiana UP, 1989. 14–26.

Rih Essed [Man of Ashes]. Directed by Nouri Bouzid. Tunisia, 1986.

Said, Edward W. *Orientalism*. New York: Vintage, 1978.

Sedgwick, Eve Kosofsky. *Epistemology of the Closet*. Berkeley: U of California P, 1990.

Stein, Elliott. Review of *Rih Essed*. *The Village Voice* 20 Jan. 1987: 95.

T.C. "Caméra de chair. Review of *Man of Ashes*. *La presse* 23 Oct. 1986.

Woodhull, Winifred. *Transfigurations of the Maghreb: Feminism, Decolonization, and Literatures*. Minneapolis: U of Minnesota P, 1993

8

THE CAMEROONIAN FILM
as Instrument of
Social and Political Change:
1991-1992

by Ekema Agbaw

The success of Bassek Ba Khobio's *Sango Malo* (1991), Jean Marie Teno's *Afrique, Je te plumerais* (1992) and Jean Pierre Bekolo's *Quartier Mozart* (1992) has once again placed Cameroonian producers among leading African film-makers. After a successful debut in the mid 1970s, Cameroonian film production seemed to have stagnated for a period of over ten years. Dikongue Pipa, Cameroon's pioneering film maker, has not produced anything significant since his award-winning *Muna Moto* (1975). Although Daniel Kamwa's *Pousse Pousse* (1975) and *Notre Fille* (1980) are still considered among the most commercially successful African films, he too has not come up with any major film since 1980 (Malkmus and Armes, 228). In order to appreciate the historical significance of *Sango Malo, Afrique, Je te plumerais* and *Quartier Mozart*, it is necessary to examine some of the factors that might have contributed to this stagnation of the Cameroonian film industry.

The prevailing social and political climate in Cameroon during the first three decades after independence from French and British colonial rule certainly contributed not only to the stagnation of Cameroonian cinema, but to the kinds of films that were produced. Despite his generally positive view of the social, economic and political developments in Cameroon during the seventies and eighties, Delancey acknowledges that "corruption and mismanagement [were] major characteristics" of a powerful bureaucracy that had been generously rewarded "with much of the material benefits of independence" (168). Bjornson's remarks about the social conditions and income distribution in Cameroon during the second decade of independence provides a much clearer picture. He shows how "the privileged class in Cameroon appropriated a disproportionate share of the country's wealth," with less than twelve percent of the total population receiving two thirds of the national income (111).

Most Cameroonian writers, musicians and film makers were either members of the privileged middle class or were aspiring to gain access to this class. Their livelihood, therefore, depended on how they represented the government and political leaders in their books, music and films. A strict government censorship forced the more outspoken writers like Mungo Beti into exile. Those who chose to stay in Cameroon and write books that were critical of the government, like Rene Philombe, were frequently in and out of jail (Philombe, 10-11). Others, like Ferdinand Oyono, whose novel *Houseboy* remains one of the most effective indictments of French colonial practices in Cameroon, and François Sengat Kuo, one of the earliest Cameroonian poets, were absorbed into the system and silenced.[1] Consequently, they ignored the injustices, corruption, financial mismanagement, abuse of power and the rise of elitism that would be troubling to the perceptive and sensitive individual. Some in this category, especially musicians, openly curried favor from the government by composing songs, writing poems or making films to praise Ahidjo. Lucien Mailli's film *Ahmadou Ahidjo, Batisseur Indefatigable de Nation Camerounais* blatantly panders to the former president for patronage (280).[2]

Those Cameroonian artists or aspiring artists who did not depend directly on the government for their livelihood disguised their criticism of government policy and practices to the point of unrecognition, or focused on issues that had little to do with political injustice and oppression of ordinary people. The sense of affluence, optimism, and well being reflected in *Pousse Pousse* came close to endorsing the official propaganda of the Ahidjo regime—that national unity and hard work would lead all Cameroonians to prosperity. Even Dikongue Pipa's *Muna Moto*, which has been widely praised for its poetic structure and flashback technique as well as its dream and fantasy sequence (Ukadike 186), does not deal with the more obvious forms of social injustice with which most Cameroonians are familiar. Rather, the movie focuses on the oppression of women through the dowry system and forced marriages. Since this practice is common to all groups in the country, particularly the peasant and working classes, no one can accuse Dikongue Pipa of criticizing the government.

By the early nineties when *Sango Malo, Afrique, Je te plumerais* and *Quartier Mozart* were produced, a lot of changes had occurred on the Cameroonian social and political landscape that might have encouraged the production of more progressive films. The dramatic increase in population, particularly in elementary and high schools, Yaounde University, and urban centers,[3] the high unemployment rate,[4] the government's failure to pay civil servants and farmers on time,[5] Biya's resistance to expanding the democratic process,[6] the continued repression, corruption and mismanagement of public resources, all combined to create a climate in which several voices provided the diagnoses and prescribed solutions for an ailing society.[7]

The three films, *Sango Malo, Afrique, Je te Plumerais* and *Quartier Mozart,* produced during the climax of what can be described in Cameroonian terms as a social revolution, are therefore not isolated historical or cultural events. They are interconnected with several other discourses by new political leaders, trade unionists, historians, musicians, playwrights, journalists and university students clamoring for change.[8]

Quartier Mozart (1992)

Of the three movies produced during 1991 and 1992, *Quartier Mozart* bears the least direct connection to the immediate social and political crisis that gripped Cameroon during the early nineties. The film's genre displays some elements of what Diawara has defined as "The return to source" genre of contemporary African cinema (159-160). Its message is less politically overt than that of *Afrique, Je te plumerais* or *Sango Malo*. It exploits traditional African beliefs in witchcraft, still strong in modern African consciousness, to expose contemporary social problems. However, its combination of fantasy and realism locates *Quartier Mozart* in the post-modern tradition.

On the surface, Bekolo seems to have used popular views about witchcraft and magic to create a world in which a young school girl, Queen of the Hood, is transformed into a boy, My Guy, by a sorceress, Mama Thekla, who herself assumes the shape of an adult male, Panka. The many practical jokes that these two characters play on their friends and acquaintances constitute the substance of the movie. Posing as a stud, My Guy seduces Samedi, the pretty daughter of the police chief, who rejects all other young men in the neighborhood as sexually inadequate. He also becomes a juicy subject of gossip for three older women who assemble at the water fountain regularly to share news about the activities in the neighborhood. The other young men in the area who accuse him of being a mercenary set up Samedi for My Guy to seduce in order to turn the police chief, Mad Dog, against him. They are confused by My Guy's apparent success with both Samedi and Mad Dog.

Panka complicates the domestic problems of Mad Dog by helping him evict his first wife, Systella. He also generates fear in the neighborhood when word goes out that he can make men's penises disappear through a simple handshake. With no clear plot or story line,

Bekolo leads the viewer through the encounters, conversations, and conflicts of these different characters and groups who come into contact with both My Guy and Panka. Much of the humor generated in the movie comes from the pranks which My Guy and Panka play on the other characters under the cover of witchcraft. This element gives *Quartier Mozart* a touch of magic realism.

The short text that introduces the movie informs us, "By the time My Guy and Panka leave, the neighborhood will never again be the same." The literal interpretation of this statement is that My Guy and Panka have transformed the neighborhood through witchcraft and sorcery. Bekolo uses contemporary African spiritual beliefs to expose those aspects of Cameroonian life that have blinded the people from recognizing their miserable social reality. The movie in effect deconstructs sex, different forms of masculine power and authority, and popular forms of entertainment.

Queen of the Hood's desire "to see what goes on underneath people's roof "can be considered the central metaphor in the movie. In a society where outward appearance is of great importance to people from all social and economic classes, it is particularly effective to use an adolescent school girl to expose what lies beneath the surface of the good life that Cameroonians seem to have enjoyed during the seventies and eighties. Cheap sex, arbitrary male power, and a wide variety of entertainments such as sports, dancing, beer drinking and even gossiping provided Cameroonians with an illusion of the "good life" which Bekolo exposes in *Quartier Morzart*.

Even before she is transformed into My Guy, Queen of the Hood discovers, through Mama Thekla's magical exposure of a sexual encounter between Atango the tailor and another young woman in the neighborhood, that people talk about sex more than they actually do it. The young woman is selling her body for a skirt she would like to have modeled after Princess Diana's. The tailor asks her to describe the type of skirt she wants. While she is describing all the details of the skirt to the tailor who is lying on top of her, Atango ejaculates even before performing the act. The young woman's disappointment is reflected in her remark "I told you we should finish doing it before talking."

The many lies that young men tell about their sexual exploits, and the false glory they enjoy over fabricated sexual conquests, become obvious to Queen once she is transformed into My Guy. As a man, My Guy will participate in conversations and activities designed to prove his masculinity. He will play checkers, play soccer, drink beer and accept the challenge to seduce Samedi to demonstrate that he is "just one of the guys." Although nothing happens between him and Samedi, My Guy lies about his sexual victory, and falsely earns the respect of Atango and the other young men "for having sex with Mad Dog's daughter." Ironically, during the encounter between the much feared police chief and My Guy, Mad Dog encourages My Guy to do whatever he is doing with Samedi, on condition that no one in the neighborhood know or talk about their relationship. The police chief's advice to his daughter and My Guy is consistent with the values of a society where most parents are aware that their teenage children are doing things in private that the parents will never acknowledge in public. Mad Dog's advice also reflects the ethics of a country where it is acceptable to embezzle public funds as long as you are not caught or leave evidence to incriminate you. Bekolo who grew up as the son of a police chief must have been acutely aware of these ambiguities in the Cameroonian value system.

Mad Dog's inability to stop the relationship between his daughter and My Guy reflects another aspect of the society which Bekolo effectively deconstructs—the power and authority of men, particularly those who have "posts" in the civil service. In his role as police chief and head of his household, Mad Dog represents public as well as private authority. At the beginning of the movie he demonstrates his wide-ranging powers by seizing the wallet of a truck pusher, taking a second wife, and warning his daughter against playing with men. Several incidents later occur in the movie that expose the limits of Mad Dog's power. In the presence of a senior relative and his tribal chief, his first wife, Systella, refuses to leave the house. In another scene, he pulls out his gun to force Systella to open her door and return his television set. At this point it becomes clear to the viewer that the only power that this much feared police chief has is the power of his gun. Bekolo generates a good deal of humor in this scene, especially when Mad Dog commands his son, who is stopping him from shooting his wife: "Allow me. I am not crazy. But if my television is not returned I will be." His reputation depends upon him being crazy, and at that moment he was acting crazed; the role between father and son is reversed, so that the son has to tame the unruly father. Yet when the door is opened, Mad Dog backs away, asking his son to stop his wife from getting too close. Unable to fire the gun that he had used to intimidate her, he seeks help from his subordinate, Viper, who advises him to resolve his domestic problems. Finally, Mad Dog turns to his night watchman, Panka, who already has a reputation for making men's penises disappear, to help him evict his wife. This entire incident, with the symbolism of the gun that cannot be fired and the penises that have disappeared, reveals the moral, psychological and sexual impotency of the men in *Quartier Mozart*.

Bekolo not only destroys the illusion that sex and power can satisfy the needs of individuals in a society that is corrupt, he also exposes the inadequacy of various forms of entertainment such as soccer, dancing, beer and gossiping which people pursue in their search for fulfillment. Soccer, which is one of the most popular recreational activities in Cameroon, becomes in *Quartier Mozart* an instrument of torture and oppression used by the other young men in the neighborhood to test My Guy's manhood. By using a series of still pictures to portray the different characters in dancing postures during the New Year Eve celebration, Bekolo seems to suggest that the characters are posing but not really dancing. Even the pleasure which the three adult women obtain from gossiping is transformed into a quarrel when it becomes clear that their stories have misrepresented the actions of certain people in the neighborhood.

The movie presents us with men whose daily conversations and actions reflect an obsession with sex and power, with women whose primary source of entertainment comes from gossiping about other people, and with a society that views soccer, beer and dancing as signs of success and good living. By deconstructing these cultural elements through a satirical comedy, Bekolo interrogates the foundations upon which Cameroonians have based their lives. The element of magic is particularly significant because it underscores the illusionary quality of those values which influence every aspect of Cameroonian life.

* * *

Afrique Je te plumerais (1992)

Viewers who prefer a more direct treatment of the subject than Bekolo provides in *Quartier Mozart* will find *Afrique, Je te plumerais* most satisfying. The film is a historical overview of how Cameroonians got to be where they are today. Teno provides the viewer with a factual account of how colonial and neo-colonial policies on politics, trade, education, publishing, civil rights and many other aspects of national life destroyed Cameroonian cultural institutions, broke the people's spirit and created a greedy ruling class that continues to aid the West in fleecing the country. The film belongs to that genre of contemporary African cinema which, according to Diawara, "puts into conflict Africans and their European colonizers" (152). Its principal action is, nevertheless, set in the present, not the past.

Afrique, Je te plumerais is not a standard documentary. The film neither presents a single perspective of the Cameroonian struggle for social and political change nor follows a linear narrative. Rather, it is a comprehensive investigation of the quest for justice and self-determination by a people whose present seems an uncanny replay of their past. By juxtaposing more recent forms of political repression under Cameroonian leaders with past colonial practices, Teno helps the viewer clearly understand how the actors might have changed, although the actions remain the same. Through several voices, including that of the producer, the movie documents the different ways Cameroonians have been oppressed, exploited and excluded from participating in key aspects of their social, economic and political life.

The images, narratives and commentaries that make up the film develop and progress around a series of "lieux de mémoire" or sites of memory. According to the French historian Pierre Nora, who coined the term in his monumental study of French historiography, "lieux de mémoire" are historical landmarks:

> where memory crystallizes and secretes itself at a particular historical moment, a turning point where consciousness of a break with the past is bound up with the sense that memory has been torn—but torn in such a way as to pose the problem of the embodiment of memory in certain sites where a sense of historical continuity persists. (Fabre & O'Meally 7)

In one way, *Quartier Mozart, Afrique, Je te plumerais* and *Sango Malo* are themselves "lieux de mémoire" because they embody "sites where a sense of historical continuity persists" for most Cameroonians. In a more general sense, the long years of European colonialism, East Cameroon's independence celebration from France on January 1, 1960, Ahmadou Ahidjo's resignation and transfer of power to Paul Biya on November 4, 1982, and the 1991 student protests and urban riots for greater democracy and a national conference, are major historical landmarks that have generated the raw material which Teno uses to compose *Afrique Je te plumerais*. These different historical events are not presented chronologically. Instead, they are juxtaposed and integrated in ways that enable the viewer to see them as one continuous struggle for justice, democracy and self-determination. At significant moments in the movie, the narrator's private memory intersects with public memory, enabling the viewer to understand how the events presented have shaped the consciousness of a particular individual.

The movie opens with a series of images that summarize the post-independent Cameroonian experience. Images of Yaounde University students throwing stones at soldiers, and opposition political leaders marching and singing "Liberté," capture the 1991 student protests and urban riots. Juxtaposed with these are images of school children marching to celebrate Cameroon's independence from France on January 1, 1960. Various images of the independence celebration, with the bright and optimistic faces of the new Cameroonian leaders, are presented. These are followed by a brief scene of students' jubilation over Ahidjo's resignation. Scenes of disillusionment under Paul Biya quickly follow, with soldiers shooting at fleeing students and the president rejecting the idea of a national conference. This prologue captures three significant historical landmarks in Cameroon during which the hopes and aspiration of the people for greater justice met with an even greater resistance to change from the government.

This cycle of hope and disillusionment in the national life or public memory is paralleled by the dreams and disappointment in the private memory of the narrator. The hustle and bustle of early morning activities in Yaounde, with petty traders setting up their stands, reminds the narrator of his own childhood dreams, which can be viewed as the dreams of every Cameroonian child: "to go to school, get a diploma, and become a wealthy civil servant." In the short poem included in this section, it is clear that the only people who matter in the society are civil servants, because if you are a civil servant, you are "somebody," "a white man." This association of significance and value with one's place in the system remains one of the greatest impediments to social progress. It has retarded the development of major sectors in the economy such as farming and small business initiatives, and it has deprived individuals who are not involved in white-collar salaried jobs from earning the respect of the society. Yet as the narrator discovers when he comes of age, not everyone can become a civil servant or obtain a white collar job. His disillusionment is paralleled by the decline of the country. In his attempt to understand why Cameroonians are experiencing so much despair in a country with abundant natural resources and a great human potential, we are shown glimpses of Cameroonians in different walks of life, particularly students, women selling food, and petty traders—people who have been excluded from the dream because they are not part of the "system."

Celestin Monga's open letter to the president, published in the December 1990 issue of *Le Messager*, provides some answers. The narrator reads excerpts of this letter which challenges the president's claim in an address to the National Assembly on December 3, 1990, that he has given Cameroonians democracy. Monga draws attention to the president's pretentious and paternalistic tone reflected in the statement "I have given you democracy," which echoes French president General Charles de Gaulle's declaration "I have given you independence." He views Biya's democracy as "bogus" in a country "where basic human rights are denied, where the majority do not have vital necessities, while a handful of opportunists divide up the spoils with impunity." He draws the president's attention to the plight of the urban population, 98% of whom "live in slums without medical care, decent food or the right to protest." He points out the marginalization of major groups—women , children, unemployed, students and peasants—from the decision-making process. As the narrator reads Monga's letter, a variety of images portraying a cross section of the marginalized population appear on the screen—secondary school students going to school, a line of writers sitting outside with their typewriters waiting for clients, school children on the playground, a petty trader carrying clothes on his head, two half naked little boys searching for food in a large dumpsite, and different images of life in the urban slums.

Monga's letter is a historical document unprecedented in the annals of Cameroon history. In a country where several people have disappeared or been jailed for simply expressing an opinion contrary to official government policy, where the official media remained the only source of information until 1990, where one of the foremost writers, Mongo Beti, stayed in exile for over thirty years because some of his novels were critical of government officials, the publication of a document that openly criticizes the president is a remarkable sign of change.

Just as the viewer is about to credit the Cameroonian government for permitting this bold demonstration of freedom of speech, we are introduced to Pius Njawe, the founder of *Le Messager*, who recounts the consequences of Monga's letter. The kidnaping of Monga on January 1, 1991, his two day detention without charges, the allegation that by publishing the open letter, Monga and Njawe showed contempt to the president, the National Assembly, and the courts, the confiscation of their passports and their subsequent trial, which resulted in the suspension of *Le Messager* and five other privately run newspapers, shattered any illusion on the part of the viewer, as it did for Cameroonians in 1991, that the current government was ready for real democracy.

However, Njawe's account as well as the images that accompany his comments reveal another element in the struggle—the Cameroonian people will not sit back and accept curtailment of their hard won freedom of the press. Njawe describes the uprising of the entire Douala population who took to the streets to demand their freedom and to protest against the blatant attack on liberty of the press. Images of a determined group of journalists marching and singing the national anthem are shown. Although this is not stated in the movie , it is important to note that this is the period when Mongo Beti returned to Cameroon through a general amnesty granted by president Paul Biya. Characteristically, Mongo Beti's scheduled talk in Yaounde Hilton Hotel in February 1991 was canceled by the government, which was uncertain as to how much freedom its citizens should have been allowed. By concluding this section of the movie with images of students marching and singing, while soldiers are standing by ready to attack, Teno skillfully captures the stalemate in the Cameroonian democratic process.

Afrique, Je te plumerais does not, however end on a pessimistic note. The comedian who is entertaining a crowd of people with his music and parody captures what can be considered a typical African attitude to oppression. The refrain of his song "When the film is sad, it makes me laugh," does not reflect cynicism towards their condition; it demonstrates the kind of humor and resilience which has enabled Africans to survive slavery, colonialism and neo-colonialism. This resilience is also evident in the image of a street vendor teaching his two children to read and write because he cannot afford to send them to school. Literacy and education are the most effective weapons to fight injustice and all forms of oppression. This is demonstrated by the University students whose education provided them with the knowledge and courage to protest for change in 1991.

* * *

Sango Malo (1991)

By focusing on the relationship and interaction between characters in a realistic social setting, *Sango Malo* reflects aesthetic as well as ideological goals. Like *Quartier Mozart*, it is pure fiction in terms of its plot, characters and actions; however, like *Afrique, Je te plumerais*, it is directly concerned with the oppression, exploitation and marginalization of ordinary people. Unlike *Afrique, Je te plumerais*, *Sango Malo* does not depend on political commentaries and historical analysis to make its point. With a clear story line and a well developed plot, the movie dramatizes the challenges faced by a young idealistic school teacher who wants to bring change in the lives of his pupils and their parents. *Sango Malo* has almost all the characteristics which Diawara identifies with the "social realist narratives." It thematizes "current sociocultural issues"; it is based on "contemporary experiences"; it opposes "tradition to modernity...agrarian and customary communities to urban and industrialized systems," while using "a traditional position to criticize and link certain forms of modernity to neo-colonialism and cultural imperialism" (141).

Through Malo's experience, Bassek Ba Khobio presents viewers with a realistic image of the social, economic and power relationships in a typical Cameroonian village. As he attempts to replace the rigid Eurocentric form of education with what he considers to be a more pragmatic African centered vocational curriculum, he employs methods and performs acts which threaten figures of authority in the village. The film develops through a series of conflicts between Malo and the different people affected by his innovations. Although Malo's conflict with the school principal is at the center of the plot, his problems with the chief, the store owner, the village catechist and his own followers, all contribute to create a microcosm of the social and political environment in which progressive Cameroonians must carry out their struggle for change. The village leadership is threatened not so much by Malo's emphasis on vocational education as they are by the self-reliant and independent spirit he encouraged in his pupils and their parents.

Most of the film's action revolves around the conflict between Malo and his new boss, the school principal. When we first see Malo in his well tailored suit, as the newly graduated teachers verify their postings on the walls of the Advanced Teachers' College, he is excited, optimistic and self confident, ready to apply the progressive theories he has acquired from college. The principal, on the other hand, is shown wearing an old-fashioned jacket, drilling the students and punishing them for failing to remember their exercises. These two opening scenes foreshadow the difficult working relationship that will exist between the bright, young teacher, full of new ideas with which he would like to experiment, and the old fox who has succeeded in the "system" by maintaining the status quo.

The most significant difference between the two men is their opposing pedagogies. Malo is casual and friendly with the students, whereas the principal relates with them as an authority figure, more to be feared than respected. The younger man emphasizes practical knowledge such as farming and carpentry to help the students acquire skills that they will need to be self-reliant adults. The older man prefers drilling exercises to enable the students to acquire knowledge that will help them to pass their final examinations. The content of Malo's lessons, including the notion of a farmer's cooperative, along with such subjects as politics, sexuality and reproduction, is relevant to the immediate experiences of the students. The principal is more concerned with imparting knowledge about France.

These differences result in several confrontations and debates between the two, with each man defending his own view of what type of education is most appropriate for African students. When Malo argues that he is providing the students with education that is adapted to their needs, the principal compares his approach with the Guinean experience under Sekou Toure during the late 1950s. The principal also seems to have the upper hand when he decides to test the students on areas over which they will be tested in the final exam. He gives them a dictation test on a passage dealing with the port of Marseilles. All the students fail. Malo's rebuttal that the children should be tested on the practical knowledge they have acquired is ignored.

This conflict is significant because it deals with the relationship between education and development in Africa. Although as the principal argues, African societies need doctors, lawyers and other highly educated people, only a very small minority succeed in passing through the educational pyramid and arriving at this level. Those who pass are ill equipped to work for the development of their various societies. Either they have acquired knowledge that they cannot apply, or no one has tried to make the different academic subjects relevant to their daily lives. The alternatives presented between the two men will either promote greater self-reliance or perpetrate dependency on the west. In a society where very few people can afford the basic necessities of life, where young people indulge in sexual relations without fully understanding the consequences of their actions, Malo provides an excellent model for the type of educational reform Africa needs. His approach reflects what Lewis C. A. Rayapen considers to be the foundation for an African philosophy of education:

> Education, then involves the liberation and the emancipation of the mind, a raising of consciousness, an inner transformation of the human being. It entails the growth of the personality as well as the acquisition of new skills for proper dominion and the improvement of self and society. (8)

Ironically, this type of education is a threat to the establishment and power structure, not only because it promotes self-reliance, freeing the people from government patronage, but also because it encourages critical thinking. As soon as people acquire the skills to relate what they learn to their own condition, they will start to ask questions and to challenge those who oppress them. Any one who is encouraging such a project must therefore be silenced or eliminated. Like most of the early African intellectuals who returned home shortly after independence to participate in building their nations, Malo is marginalized. Being transferred to the mail service of the Ministry of National Education or any other government department is like being sent to jail. He will have minimal professional contact with anyone, let alone school children. This decision by the higher authorities vindicates the principal who openly claims to have been responsible for the action.

Despite their differences, Malo and the principal can be viewed as two sides of the same coin. Malo's jeans, leather jacket and western suitcase are as alien in the village as the principal's interest in what goes on in the port of Marseilles. By virtue of their education, the two men are products of an alien culture. In Malo, the principal is also reminded of his own stubborn behavior as a young teacher. Through a conversation with his wife we learn that he would have liked one of his own children to be like Malo. As he tells his wife, he does not completely disagree with some of the things Malo is doing with the students. Rather, he disapproves of Malo's arrogant attitude. This is demonstrated by his admiration of the students when they are shown working on the farm under the supervision of a different teacher who happens to be Malo's wife. He accepts a pineapple from the farm, presented to him as a gift. Despite his several fights with Malo, he declines to join the chief and store owner in their complaint against the young man.

One way to explain Bassek's portrayal of these two characters and their ambivalent relationship is to view each as a representative of a different generation of the Cameroonian educated class. The principal represents the first generation of the Cameroonian elite who took over from the colonial masters. The more radical members of this group, those who demanded real independence with a truly democratic government, were killed, jailed or forced into exile. Others who were more pragmatic or self-cententered, depending on whom you talk to, became part of the "system" and helped to extend colonial oppression and exploitation for several years after independence. Malo's principal belongs to this group. In Malo, he sees the rebellious and independent spirit he once had. Although he admires this spirit, he is also threatened by it. This threat becomes real when the chief suggests that Malo wants his "post." In Cameroon, as in many other African countries, most people cannot separate themselves from their public functions. The position as head of the school belongs to the principal. For him, it is like a political post that he has worked hard to win. He will therefore get rid of anyone, as he does Malo, who tries to take this "post" away from him. He is like a president for life.

Malo, on the other hand, belongs to a generation of educated Cameroonians who cannot be bought, partly because there is too little for too many, but also because those in his parents' generation do not want to relinquish their "posts." Malo can tear up the letter transferring him to the mail service of the Ministry of National Education and resign from the civil service because he knows that his salary cannot sustain him in Yaounde. Desperate and disillusioned young men like Malo led the social protest in Yaounde, Douala, Garoua, Bamenda, Victoria and Kumba. Those in this group may not be less power hungry than their predecessors, as Malo later demonstrates in his management of the cooperative, they just have fewer options.

Malo's conflict with the chief exposes another area of national life that needs to be changed—the rampant abuse of power, evident in *Quartier Mozart* and *Afrique, Je te plumerais*. As an administrative auxiliary appointed by the government, the chief is under no obligation to serve the people or protect their interests. While part of his income comes from a small government allowance, a large part is derived from extorting the villagers through arbitrary taxes and forced gratuities. Favorable reports from a chief generally improve the chances of a civil servant applying for a promotion. By ordering Malo to make his students provide wood to the chief, the principal will continue to remain in the chief's good books. We see the chief threatening a palm wine tapper with higher taxes when he delays offering the chief wine or money for favors rendered the previous year.

Malo, therefore, commits a grievous crime by not acknowledging the chief. He neither brings the chief a present nor pays him homage when he arrives in the village. When invited by the chief who sees him on the road with his students, Malo is impatient and nonchalant. He shows more interest in his students than in the chief. Under normal circumstances, a chief should be impressed by a young teacher who is anxious to be with his students; however, in a society where flattering or ingratiating oneself with authority figures is considered more important than serving the public, Malo's attitude is a violation of an important social etiquette.

His most serious act against the chief is establishing the cooperative. Such an organization empowers the people and weakens the Chief's authority over them. Not only will his power diminish, he will also lose a significant part of his livelihood if he can no longer extort money and gifts from them. It is not surprising that the chief denounces the cooperative idea and brands it an act of political ambition. His complaint to the sub-prefect does not discourage Malo from going ahead with his idea. When later, Big Eyes, the village gossip, tells Malo how Ella's parents were killed shortly after independence because her father was a trade unionist who tried to establish a cooperative, we are again reminded of how much government authorities are threatened by grass roots, self-help initiatives.

The store owner, who represents the economic power in the village, is the one most affected by the changes which Malo is bringing to the community. He represents the small group of businessmen in Cameroon who acquired great wealth by obtaining the exclusive rights to import and sell much needed commodities. He has such a monopoly in the village because no one else can raise the money to establish another store. When Malo arrives, his business is booming, his prices are arbitrary, and his attitude towards his customers is disrespectful. But Malo's ideas become a great challenge to the store owner. When a village woman who has been cheated by the storekeeper complains to her husband, her son, who has been influenced by Malo's teachings, advises her to boycott the store. When the store owner physically assaults a school girl who protests his high prices, the store is ransacked by Malo's students. Once Malo establishes the cooperative, he destroys the store owner's monopoly, forcing him to import prostitutes from town to revitalize his business.

Malo's conflict with the village catechist is not as explosive as that with the principal, the chief and the store owner. It is, nevertheless, significant because the catechist represents the religious power in the village. Until recently, with the Pope's appointment of Cardinal Christian Tumi as the head of the Catholic church in Cameroon, the church maintained its close alliance with the government established during the colonial period.[9] This alliance facilitated colonialism by helping to pacify the people with religious ideals. The Catholic church helped the post-independence government to consolidate power by presenting opposition groups as ungodly communists. Political leaders and civil servants paid lip service to the church in order to maintain their jobs or to get promoted. In *Sango Malo*, the chief and the principal sit in front of the church while the catechist is preaching. Malo, on the other hand is jogging when almost everyone in the village is in church. The store owner, on his part, bribes the catechist with gifts of sugar and kerosene when the catechist condemns his use of prostitutes to promote his business. Consequently, the catechist joins the chief in denouncing Malo's idea of establishing a cooperative. By branding the cooperative as a communist venture, the catechist uses the same strategy that Catholic clergy had used to help the Ahidjo government to tar the UPC opposition.

The combined resistance of the principal, the chief, the store owner and the catechist would never have stopped Malo from transforming the social, economic and political life of the village if he had not alienated his own followers. Unfortunately, like most revolutionaries, Malo is short-sighted in two significant areas. While empowering the people, he fails to appreciate the depth and complexity of their minds. Through a democratic process, he succeeds in forming the cooperative, although some people vote against the project. When later some of those who originally opposed the idea want to join, he rejects their membership without putting the matter to a vote. As one of the members point out, his action contradicts the very idea of a cooperative.

He also fails to recognize those aspects of their lives that the people do not want to change. The people respond positively to the adult literacy classes where he teaches members of the cooperative French names of common food items and cash crops. But he is viewed as a dictator when he tells them that they cannot seek pleasure in beer and women to escape their sad reality. By refusing to pay a dowry when he marries a girl from the village, Malo is again forcing change against the people's will.

It is this conflict with his followers, which comes to a climax when he insists on establishing the cooperative farm in the sacred forest, that finally leads to Malo's downfall. Since the sacred forest is considered to be the resting place of ancestral spirits, Malo's agenda for change threatens to destroy that which is dear to the people. Besides the disillusioned village gossip, Big Eyes, no one joins Malo when he decides to clear the sacred forest. When the military police, led by the chief and the store owner, come to arrest him, the village people stand by and watch without putting up a resistance in Malo's defense. At that moment, they are as relieved as the chief to be rid of him.

Sango Malo is successful not simply because of its realistic plot, but also because it brings together in a simple story almost every segment of Cameroonian society—the political leader, government bureaucrats, law enforcement officers, a village chief, a school administrator, a school teacher, a college student, school children, a village belle, a school drop-out, a local clergyman, prostitutes and peasants. The settings in which the film's actions occur are also realistic and typical—the school, the chief's house, a government office, a provision store/bar, and farming areas. All these settings are public spheres where individuals, mostly men, are constantly negotiating power relations. Even the cooperative that Malo sets up to establish an egalitarian group becomes another terrain in the constant struggle for power.

The people give little or no importance to domestic relationships. Whenever we see a man and a woman or a husband and a wife interacting, the man is always trying to assert his authority over the woman. This is the case in the relationship between the principal and his wife, the chief and his concubine, the parents of Malo's wife, and even between Malo and his wife. The film demonstrates how this private sphere of social life—gender relationships—has been neglected in Cameroonian society. Ironically, with all his progressive ideas, even Malo imposes his western values on his fiancee by refusing to pay the dowry. When his father-in-law commits suicide as a result of the humiliation, Malo cannot deal with the domestic crisis. Instead of taking responsibility and comforting his wife with reassurances of his love, he leaves her at home lamenting and takes refuge in planning the affairs of the cooperative. Power politics in the public sphere becomes an escape for men who lack the emotional capacity to meet the needs of their wives and children.

One of the most memorable moments in the movie is the scene where school children invade the public space from which they are excluded, by ransacking the village store. This spontaneous act of defiance shows the contribution that the most disempowered members of the society can make to bring about social change. It also reflects the rioting and looting that occurred in some of Cameroon's major cities during 1991, the year when the movie was made.

Despite Sango Malo's short sightedness, the movie celebrates the idealism and personal sacrifice of a young school teacher who gives up his government salary and stays in the village to work for change. Malo's vision to enable the people to achieve self-reliant, grass roots development, the courage of helpless women and children who rise against their exploiter, and the confidence of peasants who continue the social and economic revolution even without a leader, constitute effective models of how real change can be achieved in African societies such as Cameroon.

* * *

It is certainly not a coincidence that three film-makers working independently of each other would produce films that, though significantly different in their form and content, deal with the same issue, a people's struggle for social and political change. It is even more remarkable that the three films were produced within a period of two years, 1991-92, when the Cameroonian people rose up in protest for social justice and greater democracy as they have never done since the fight for independence from French colonial rule.

Some may interpret the slow economic recovery in Cameroon following several months of civil disobedience or "villes mortes" in 1991,[10] the government's ability to crush the urban uprising after the 1992 presidential elections and Biya's recent re-election for a seven years term,[11] as signs that the revolution failed. There are, however, many indicators that the government is responding to the people's demand for change. These includes the number of multi-party elections which have been held in Cameroon since 1991, the increased number of representatives from opposition political parties in parliament, and Cameroon's desire to join the British commonwealth. Regardless of how one chooses to interpret the last six years of Cameroonian history, *Sango Malo*, *Quartier Mozart*, and *Afrique, Je te plumerais* will remain historical monuments to remind successive generations of Africans that without guns it is possible to wage an effective war against the forces of oppression. Not only have these films become important "sites of memory," they have identified major areas which future reformers must address in the continuous struggle to liberate Africans from the shackles of imperialism and modern forms of slavery.

NOTES

1. For several years, Oyono served as Cameroonian Ambassador to the United Nations, and later to France. He later became a government minister in the Biya regime. Sengat Kuo served in both the Ahidjo and the Biya governments as senior minister. Even Bernard Fonlon who was often critical of the government showered praises on Ahidjo in the 1978 issue of *ABBIA* (6-7).

2. As Bjornson points out, the film was shown throughout Cameroon during the 1978 commemoration of Ahidjo's twenty years in power. Mailli's exaggerated praise of Ahidjo was, however, not much different from what internationally acclaimed musicians like Manu Dibango, Eboa Lottin and the then popular Cameroonian musician in Nigeria, Nico Mbarga, did in a grand musical concert at the Yaounde Sports stadium to celebrate the same occasion.

3. In 1976, Cameroon's population was estimated to be 9.5 million with annual growth rate of 2.7 percent. But a significant part of the population, the urban dwellers, who led the struggle for change in 1991 grew at an annual rate of 7.5 percent (Delancey, 84-85).

4. For most of the sixties and seventies, every university graduate was hired immediately or admitted into some Grande Ecole. By the early eighties, Ahidjo initiated, and Biya continued the "Mille Cinq Cent" policy designed to hire fifteen hundred university graduates every year. This could not, however, solve the growing unemployment problem among high school graduates who failed the BAC or the G.C.E. examinations, and university graduates who did not make the "Mille Cinq Cent" list.

5. During 1991, civil servants' salaries were consistently late by at least one month. For several months, farmers did not receive payments for sale of their cash crops.

6. On November 4, 1982, President Ahidjo surprised Cameroonians and the world by resigning as head of state and appointing his prime minister, Paul Biya, to succeed him (Ngoh, 300). The people's hope for greater democracy was shattered by a series of repressive measures undertaken by the new regime to curb dissent.

7. In early 1990, Yondo Black, then President of the Cameroon Bar Association and a few other people were tried and sentenced to jail for planning to form an opposition political party. On May 6, 1990, several journalists working for Cameroon Radio Television (CRTV) and some Yaounde university professors were arrested and jailed for speaking in support of a multi-party democracy in the program "Cameroon Calling." Three weeks later, on May 26, 1990, Ni John Fru Ndi and Ben Muna announced the formation of a new political party, the Social Democratic Front (SDF). Eight people were killed by soldiers in Bamenda, during the rally launching the SDF.

8. A series of presidential decrees promulgated on December 19, 1990, established the freedom of the press, and authorized the formation of other political

parties to compete with the ruling Cameroon Peoples Democratic Movement (CPDM). The same laws allowed political prisoners to be liberated and exiles to return home. Within a few months, more than fifty new parties emerged with different agendas for the nation. Popular musicians like La Piro de Mbanga conveyed the sentiments of the disenfranchised masses through their music, while playwrights like Bole Butake and Bate Besong used theatre to contribute to the national dialogue on the state of Cameroon. Privately run newspapers became one of the few lucrative businesses in a country where banks and many other commercial enterprises were failing.

9. Christian Tumi, an anglophone, is the first Cameroonian to be appointed cardinal. Since his appointment on June 28, 1988, he has been openly critical of government corruption and repression.

10. Between April and August 1991, opposition parties organized a campaign of civil disobedience to force President Paul Biya to convene a national conference. While most civil servants continued to work, economic activities in Cameroon's urban centers were brought to a standstill. The university and many secondary schools were closed.

11. In October 1997, President Biya was re-elected for a seven year term in an election that was boycotted by major opposition parties.

9

LA HAINE,
or Culture Wars in Paris
and the *Banlieues*

by Stephen Zacks

One evening during the student strikes in the winter of 1995, an incident occured whose representation in the press hints at the cultural perception of the youth and the tenor of the relationship between the city of Paris and the outlying suburban regions, referred to in general as *les banlieues*, or in other contexts, *les cités*. On a typical day, protesters would march through the 5th arrondissement passing the various campuses of the University of Paris, from the Grande Sorbonne along rue de l'Université to the Jussieu campus, down rue Linné and St. Geoffrey Hilaire to Censier, and past the Pantheon and the Faculté de Droit.

This particular day the march came to a halt in front of the Jussieu pavillion, where protesters had turned over three cars in the middle of the street, blocking off the road. When the CRS (Compagnie Républicaine de Sécurité, the semi-military riot police) arrived decked in riot gear, the students had barricaded the gates of the pavillion and, as the evening progressed, began looting with impunity, destroying research laboratories, the bookstore, the cafeteria, and lighting bonfires on the pavillion. The campus guards hid in their booths, and the CRS, legally prohibited from entering the campus without permission from the dean, waited in formation at both ends of the road.

The innuendos buried in an article the following day in *France Soir* must have in some measure confirmed the prejudices of the general public. A photo in which several people in a crowd of protesters wore scarves and hats to hide their faces was accompanied by a caption that read: "Les étudiants qui manifestaient ont été *infiltrés* par des *casseurs...*" [The students who were protesting were infiltrated by looters]. The article concluded on this note, quoting a statement from a "*voyou*" [rogue]:

> Cela me fait plaisir de voir la haine qui sort, cela me fait du bien, expliquait
> un casseur, ce matin sur Europe 1. Ce n'est pas uniquement le vandalisme

pour le vandalisme. Evidemment il y a un petit peu de "fun", mais il y a aussi des raisons politiques. Il y a des choses qui ne vont pas en France dans les banlieues. (*France-Soir*, Dec. 1, 1995)

[It makes me happy to see the hate emerging, it does me good, explained a looter this morning on Europe 1. It is not just vandalism for vandalism's sake. Clearly there is a little bit of "fun" involved, but there are also political motivations. Things are not right in France's suburbs.]

I was living in Jussieu at the time, and this episode represented my introduction to the question of the *banlieues* in France. It struck me that the suppressed racial issues implicit in the terms *banlieue*, *casseur*, and *voyou* bear a close similarity to the way in which racial issues in the United States are indirected denoted by terms like "inner city" and by reference to the names of locales specifically associated with minority groups. British scholars have been compelled to ask the question at a recent conference: "Are American-style Ghettos Emerging in Europe?" It was not until I returned to the United States that I viewed Kassovitz's film, and it had the impact of crystallizing all of the unconscious cultural understandings embedded in the language and society to suggest a way of talking about this question.

La Haine

Originally titled "Droit de cité" in an effort to assuage the fears of magistrates whose permission was necessary to film on location, *La Haine*, written and directed by Mathieu Kassovitz, the son of a TV film director, is ostensibly a film about police brutality against young Beurs (Arabs born in France) and other immigrants of African origin. The film, shot documentary-style in black and white, uses the tools of social realism to narrate 24 hours in the life of three Parisian *"banlieusards."* The narrative is set in the wake of a riot sparked by an incident of police brutality [*bavure policière*] in which Abdel, a Beur, was severely beaten while in police custody. With its popular soundtrack featuring music by French gangster rap artists such as Assassin, the film became a fetish reference for journalists reporting events affecting immigrants, the youth, and the suburbs. Henceforth any article concerning *"les cités"* would almost inevitably make reference to *La Haine*.

While I am likewise compelled to relate *La Haine* to my own personal experiences in France in a commonsensical manner, it seems to me that such a pattern of criticism, like the use of references to the film to add color to journalistic reporting, contributes to a fundamental confusion between the text and the sociological reality: the film and reality are referred to as if they were contiguous and as if the film were a transparent representation of reality. Such "naturalized" readings, engendered in particular by films of the social realist genre, threaten to collapse the difference between fiction and documentary as narrative forms. Indeed, many of the conventions of the film encourage such a confusion. I take seriously, however, Kassovitz's statement that *La Haine* is a fiction film, and does not pretend to represent the reality of the French *banlieues*, or to speak for the French youth (Kassovitz: screenplay). It is not uncoincidental that after *Do the Right Thing,* Spike Lee was asked to do precisely this with regard to black experience, so that the questions posed by his extremely complex film were dissolved by the consequent rhetoric, and the films he has since directed have often appeared to be lost in a reaction to these expectations. The docu-fictional text, a manufactured cultural product par excellence, disappears into the social reality from which it was constructed, and both the analytic value and whatever artistic originality it may have possessed are gradually drawn away and banalized, submitted to the prevailing social order from which fiction, as an artistic form, needs to distance itself in order to function. Consequently, methodological questions arise for film criticism, such as how to uncouple the text from the sociological reality that it presents so as to understand the function and logic of the symbols and ideological messages. But to what extent does the meaning of the film depend on an assumed cultural understandings of the sociological reality, and what specific features of the political and sociological context inform the meaning? The failure to critically evaluate the work of art in this context, particularly when the work is so evidently grounded in social and political realities, is tantamount to its reduction to the referential function of such discursive forms as journalism, sociology, and documentary.

Three contentious aspects of contemporary French culture are crystallized in *La Haine*: postcoloniality, characterized by the influence of former colonial subjects on the culture of the colonial power; the social structural disinvestment of youth and consequent emergence of a distinct marginal identity separate from the sociocultural "center"; and globalization or Americanization, most evident in the influx of American products, words, expressions, technical terms, and cultural references, as a result of which unlikely manifestations of cultural syncretization take place. These relatively recent historical developments form the sociological backdrop of *La Haine*, and are reflected in the physical locations, narrative, characterization, and dialogue, as well as the cinematography, soundtrack, and style of the film. Rather than treat different aspects of world culture as isolated categories and impose them on the film, I organize my analysis around the formal structures of the film by deploying the traditional tools of literary criticism, such as setting, theme, and language, revamped for a sociological treatment of the specificities of docu-fictional film, and incorporate the idea of world culture as a device to locate the text within the present historical moment in order, ultimately, to create an analytic distance from it.

Postcoloniality and la Banlieue.

> La Haine n'est pas un film sur la banlieue. Ce ne sont pas les arabes ou les noirs contre la police, c'est une certaine jeunesse des cités. Dans la police aussi, il y a des noirs, des arabes, des blancs. Mais les deux se voient comme des icones. Les flics voient les jeunes de banlieue comme des icones et inversement. (Kassovitz, screenplay)

> [Hate is not a film about the suburbs. It is not simply a question of Arabs or blacks against the police, but of a certain sort of youth from the projects. There are blacks, Arabs, and whites among the police as well. But the two sides see each other as icons; the police see the youth from the suburbs as icons and the converse.]

La Haine is set in a fictional housing project called Les Muguets, presumably named after Les Minguettes, the government project in Lyon from which the Beur movement originated in 1983, when North African immigrants from the *cité* led a march to President Mitterand's office under the banner of "pour légalité et contre le racisme" (Begag, 1990) [for equality and against racism]. The film was actually shot on location in a half-finished HLM (*hébergement à loyer modéré* [low-cost housing project]), constructed in the 1970s for workers at a nearby auto plant, located in the Noë ghetto of Chanteloup les Vignes, a wine-making village northwest of Paris.

In the screenplay, the opening sequence is described in this way: "Un jeune beur d'une vingtaine d'années se tient immobile au milieu de la cité et regarde droit devant lui: à une dizaine de mètres, des CRS barrent l'horizon..." [A young Beur in his twenties stands immobile in the middle of the projects and looks straight ahead: some ten meters away riot police block the horizon.] From the first frames an opposition is initiated between the police and youth. At first Kassovitz's rhetoric stance seems unambiguously clear; the police and the youth form a structural opposition which will find its denouement in tragedy. Nevertheless, to his credit, the film does not degenerate into a simple diatribe against the police, nor does the film turn entirely on this simplistic opposition. Instead, the film seems to continually extend and expand upon a sense of the diversity of possible relationships existing in the *banlieues*, not only between the youth and the police, but between parents and children, among siblings, and between friends, all of whose structural positions, complicity, and efforts at resistance contribute to the process of ghettoization.

In the second sequence, a satellite image of the globe is accompanied by the following voice-over, which is repeated twice in the film (with a slight variation during the last repetition), and serves to frame the narrative as a whole:

> C'est l'histoire d'un homme qui tombe d'un building de cinquante étages. A chaque étage, au fur et à mesure de sa chute, il se répéte pour sans cesse se rassurer: "Jusqu'ici tout va bien, jusqu'ici tout va bien, jusqu'ici tout va bien..." L'important ce n'est pas la chute, c'est l'atterrissage. (*La Haine* 1995)

> [It's the story of a man who falls from the fiftieth floor of a skyscraper. To reassure himself, as he passes each floor, he repeats to himself over and over again, "So far so good, so far so good, so far so good..." But what counts is not the fall, it's the landing.]

The anecdote immediately evokes a sense of the relationship between the fall of the individual and the failure of society. The subsequent image of a Molotov cocktail exploding mid-air as it falls to earth extends the metaphor further so that finally what is at stake is the status of civilization and the well-being of the entire world. The rhetoric of the sequence suggests that the future of French civilization, and by extension, the future of the world depends upon the consequences of the struggle of a few kids in a Parisian housing project.

Other examples of this rhetoric are evident. As Vinz, Sayid, and Hubert ride the train into Paris, the image of the globe reappears on a billboard reading "Le Monde est à vous." [The world is yours.] Hubert closes his eyes as if to hold back tears. (Later one of them effaces an identical billboard by spray-painting "nous" in the place of "vous.") Here the official compaign to provide inspiration for the youth is set against the hopelessness of the individual protagonist. In the following scene Vinz and Sayid stand on a balcony above the traffic of the city; the camera zooms; the city rushes up behind their backs and seems to engulf them. The youths are dramatically placed in relief against the indifferent traffic of the city and its edifices. In effect, the protagonists are not only to be positioned in opposition to the police, but as representatives of the social reality of France as opposed to official or public representations of French culture, French civil society versus the French state.

When the framing anecdote of *la chute* recurs the second time, Hubert, Sayid, and Vinz are stranded in Paris. As they sit on a rooftop looking out on Paris, the Tour Eiffel in the distance, Hubert recounts the anecdote. "C'est comme nous à la cité," he concludes, "pour l'instant tout va bien." [It's like us in the projects; for the moment everything is O.K.] The Tour

Eiffel functions as a visual counterpoint, opposing an official representation of French culture to the marginalized individual. When Sayid snaps his fingers, the light of the Eiffel Tower goes out; however, this occurs only after he turns his back. The joke about Hollywood cinema becomes in part a joke on the protagonist himself. If the authority of official culture is (symbolically) subverted, the individual is not conscious of his agency or of the effect of his presence on official culture. By juxtaposing the symbols of French civilization and the youth from the *banlieues*, such visual jokes are suggestive of the complex relationship between individuals and social structures. Culture appears larger than life to the marginalized individual, but paradoxically, such a position turns out to be a privileged site of resistance, and consequently, of the emergence of new forms of culture.

A History of Police Brutality.

On 6 April 1993 police in the 18th arrondissement of Paris arrested three youths, two of them minors, who were reportedly stealing cigarettes. There is a large immigrant population in this area and the inhabitants complain of incessant police identity checks and generally insensitive policing. One of the youths arrested was 17-year-old Makomé M'Bowole, born in Zaire. He was taken to the Grandes-Carrières police station where he was interviewed by a detective constable. After two hours Makomé M'Bowole was placed in custody (garde à vue) and the Prosecutor was informed in accordance with the standard procedure. At around noon, the Prosecutor ordered the lifting of the custody for the two minors. One was released shortly after his parents had been contacted; apparently Makomé M'Bowole's parents could not be contacted. The officer continued his interrogation and at around 5pm shot and killed the minor. According to statement he and other officers made to members of the IGS, who conducted an internal inquiry, Makomé M'Bowole had verbally threatened the officer who then took his handgun from a drawer and placed it against Makomé M'Bowole's temple; the gun went off. After the shooting the officer was reported as saying, "I wanted to frighten him" (Amnesty, 1994).

La France est une République indivisible, laïque, démocratique et sociale. Elle assure l'égalité devant la loi de tous les citoyens sans distinction d'origine, de race ou de religion. (Article 2, Constitution of 1958.)

[France is an indivisible, secular, democratic, and social republic. It guarantees the equality before the law of all citizens without distinction with regard to origin, race, or religion.]

The 1994 Amnesty International report on human rights abuses by French law enforcement officers documented 11 cases of immigrant youths shot and killed by police officers in the space of 18 months. The death of Makomé M'Bowole was one of the most infamous incidents, and the circumstances of Makomé's death and the events surrounding his killing, which inspired Kassovitz to make *La Haine*, form the basis of the film's narrative structure. As the opening credits appear, footage of the riots that followed the death of Makomé is accompanied by the Bob Marley song "Burning and Looting"; later in the film, Makomé's name appears spray-painted onto a wall in the background. This explicit use of cultural references is an important way in which the film links the narrative to the social reality of contemporary France.

Kassovitz makes a point of showing the police as complex, made up of many different classes, ethnicities, ages, and personalities. It should be noted that there is a fundamental distinction between the CRS and the civilian police force: the CRS are a paramilitary force, whose primary function is to serve the state in maintaining social order. This is the monolithic force we see during the opening credits, when rioters are throwing rocks at officers decked out in helmets, shields, and rifles.The purpose of the modern civilian police force, which is supposed to be made up of members of civil society themselves, is in principle to "protect and serve" the people. These are the officers like the ones who break up the roof-top cook-out: the older officer, a prototypical member of the working class, who appeals to universal values, respect for authority, and French cultural norms, ordering them to get off the roof in "la joie et la bonne humeur," as well as the Arab one, who wants them to see him as one of them, tries to identify with them, and knows their names.

At the hospital they encounter a younger officer who asks them not to cause trouble for him, says that he is just doing his job, and has trouble asserting his authority, in addition to an authoritarian one (a black) who grabs Sayid, calling him the ring-leader (*le chef*), and places him under arrest. In central Paris there is an officer who uses the "vous" form in addressing Sayid ("Putain, ils sont polits, les keufs, ici," says Sayid, "carrément il me dit vous et tout." [Fuck, pigs are polite here! They even say "may I."]) in addition to perversely abusive ones, who take Hubert and Sayid into custody, tie them up and racially insult and torture them. The effect of this should be to diffuse the sense of binary opposition, yet the film culminates in an image of the most extreme polarization. The contradictory representations are important to the anti-polemical point the film ultimately makes, one which would be undermined by looking at the film from a "vulgar" structuralist perspective. Indeed, though the film certainly depends on oppositions, in important ways it also serves to defuse them.

The film could, in this respect, be seen to function as a critique of the conceptual categories that might lend credence to racist ideologies. At least we would be justified in asserting that the competing characterizations help the film to succeed as fiction, and gives the dialogue depth: "La majorité des flics dans la rue ne sont pas là pour vous taper; ils sont pour vous protéger," [The majority of the cops in the streets aren't there to beat you; they're there to protect you] says the friendly officer. "Hé oui," says Hubert, "mais qui va nous protéger de vous?" [Yeah, but who is going to protect us from you?]

Even though the film is not primarily an anti-racist polemic, the film does accord with a certain tradition in France, well-established by the years of socialist political ascendency, of dealing with immigrants as a sociological problem, and consequently to directly address the social and political conditions, the repressive forces, and the economic limitations to which they are subjected. One of the primary components of ghettoization in the American context (as well as in the German-Jewish context in which the word has its origin) apart from the matrix of sociological conditions that contribute to stagnation and isolation, is an ideology of otherness, in which the ghetto become representative of a distinct cultural reality, with its own language, system of exchange, underground economy, and identity.

This subculture, not yet articulated in the reactionary language of ghetto separatism, is what I will attempt to identify in what follows. Its ideology is not fundamentally at odds with the ideals of the Fifth Republic; it clearly resonates in many ways with a concept of pluralistic nationality that has strong roots in France, in contrast to the blood-and-soil ideology manifested in the ideals of the National Front, the policies of Pasqua, and other anti-immigrant political tendencies. That said, there are obvious rumblings of a racist reaction to be found among Kassovitz's youths: watching a man come down an escalator at Les Halles, Hubert stereotypes him as the kind of common French person carried along by the system, who votes for the right but denies being racist. As the man passes, Sayid hisses bitterly, "Racist!"

"L'Argot" de Banlieue.

> L'argot n'est pas une forme séparée de la langue, il en est simplement une des formes, constituant une de ses variétés, et son existence est le signe que la société est divisée en groupes, en "tribus," qui chacun marque de son sceau la langue générale. (Calvet, 1993)

> [Argot is not a separate form of language, it is simply one the forms constituting one of its varieties, and its existence is the sign that the society is

> divided into groups, into tribes, each of which marks the general language
> with a seal.]

> Le recours à tout terme étranger ou à toute expression étrangère est prohibé
> lorsqu'il existe une expression ou un terme français de même sens, en
> particulier une expression ou un terme approuvé dans les conditions prévues
> par les dispositions réglementaires relative à l'enrichissement de la langue
> française. (Projet de loi de 1994 relatif à l'emploi de la langue française;
> Sanders, 1993)

> [The use of any foreign term or any foreign expression is prohibited so long as
> there exists a French expression or term with the same sense, in particular an
> expression or term that has been approved under the conditions provided for in
> the regulatory clauses concerning the enrichment of the French language.]

Nowhere is the tension between the official representation of French culture and the social reality as signified by second-generation immigrant youths more apparent than in the use of language. The language spoken in *La Haine* is identifiable by any French speaker as a language specific to the youth, especially those living in the suburbs. *Verlan*, a form of coded speech in which the syllabic order of individual words is reversed, though it existed prior to the development of a distinct suburban underclass, has reemerged as a marker of identity for contemporary youth. Not only does it distinguish the younger generation from adults, but embedded in its codes is the distinction between urban and suburban, as well as differences among dwellers of suburban "zones" themselves, who frequently coin their own characteristic *verlan* terms. *Verlan* words such as *meuf* (*femme* [woman]), *keuf* (*flic* [cop]), and *Beur* (*Arabe*), *relou* (*lourd* [a drag]), used repeatedly in *La Haine*, are widely used in the suburban ghettos, and mark a general social distinction between inhabitants of urban centers and those from the margins.

The scene in which Hubert, Vinz, and Sayid find themselves at an opening in an art gallery provides a good study of the contrast between these two speech communities. Initially, when the three *banlieusards* enter the gallery, they are not set apart from the others in any way except, possibly, by their dress, and are assumed to belong to the group. They are offered beverages and hors d'oeuvres, and while they evidently have difficulty relating to the art work ("C'est affreux!" says Sayid [It's frightful!]) race is certainly not an issue. The conflict begins when Sayid becomes interested in a métisse woman and asks Hubert to approach her on his behalf. She is willing to meet him, and openly receives the proposition of being introduced. Before long, however, Sayid's mode of expression comes up against standards of behavior with which he is apparently unfamiliar: "T'es bonne," ("You're hot") he says. As the conflict begins to deepen and attention is being drawn to them, one of the young women says, "On veut bien parler avec vous, mais toute de suite vous êtes aggressifs! Comment vous voulez qu'on vous respecte?" [We are perfectly willing to talk to you but right away you attack us! How do you expect us to respect you?]

The point is not merely that Sayid's form of address is impolite, itself a concept that, particularly in France, is deeply connected to what are assumed to be commonly-held values, norms, and standards, but that he is embedded in a subjectivity that assumes a common linguistic understanding, and this understanding is completely at odds with the norms of the center. At the very least we may conclude that linguistic differences play an important role in the protagonists' inability to cope with the urban center, and that the film does represent differences in codes of speech and behavior. The location of this difference carries with it an implicit analysis of the character of the foreignness of the suburban dweller vis à vis the urban center, a difference rooted for Kassovitz in social isolation rather than ethnic difference—though ethnic difference is shown in the family backgrounds of the protagonists. The banlieuesard is different because he is a ghettoized; he is not ghettoized because he is different.

Although not especially salient in *La Haine*, if there is a tendency for the language of the youth to reflect ethnic roots, American rather than North African speech styles and cultural references set them apart from others. Indeed, the use of Americanisms to punctuate sentences is quite common in the suburban argot. To return to the quote from the Jussieu *casseur*, "Evidemment il y a un petit peu de 'fun,'" he says. It is difficult to explain this tendency without reference to the notion of world culture, a culture dominated by the English language. The American invasion has been the object of linguistic policies developed to compensate for the inroads of foreign words into the French language, as well as radio programming quotas that require a minimum percentage of time to be devoted to French artists (as opposed to Francophone artists).

Studies of the language use of second-generation immigrants have observed an almost total neglect of the language of origin; indeed, the language of the *banlieues* does not reflect distinctions between ethnic identities so much as the difference between regional subcultures. The appropriation of English words and Americanisms as an idiom for the expression of protest is intimately connected to an idealized notion of America with roots in popular cultural representations that obscure or gloss over persistent social divisions. In this respect, when we see Hollywood films and listen to music, we should be aware that we are, to a large extent, dealing with an American export. In the case of French rap, with rare exceptions such as MC Solaar, the musical expressions closely mimic those of American artists, especially Public Enemy. If, apart from its gangster rap ethos, the language employed in *La Haine* does not conform to sociolinguistic expections in terms of the importation of the English language, the MTV film language employed by Kassovitz, not to mention the film/soundtrack marketing scheme, could almost be likened to import substitution.

Products of World Culture

> Outside and inside form a dialectic of division, the obvious geometry of which blinds us as soon as we bring it into play in metaphorical domains. (Bachelard, *The Poetics of Space*)

> Écarte Descartes et toutes les philosophies
> Étudie les lois universelles de la vie
> Une seule option, pour cette action
> Soyons la division, contre la division

> (MC Solaar, "La musique adoucit les mœurs" [Music softens morals])

> [Put aside Descartes and all the other philosophies
> Study the universal laws of life
> The only option for this practice
> Be division, against division]

In his recent history of post-war France, Robert Gildea points out that in the wake of World War II, American aid for post-war reconstruction under the Marshall plan was exchanged for specific economic privileges, one of the main beneficiaries of which was the American film industry. In the post-war years, American films consistently dominated the French market, protected by trade agreements. Thus, a youth growing up in post-war France will have been brought up to a large extent on American culture. In reflecting on this context, one cannot help be reminded of the fact that the Nouvelle Vague was directly reacting to the dominant conventions of Hollywood cinema, a cinema so familiar to French audiences that the avant-garde itself almost became popular.

In contrast to the free rein granted internationally to American film distribution, the French film industry can be said to have remained primarily national. Funding for French film comes almost exclusively from the government, channelled through various public institutions that inevitably have certain particular interests; observers of African cinema have often lamented the fact that French funding privileges certain representations of African culture, sometimes far removed from popular sensibilities. The tendency in French film of the 1980s, continuing in the 1990s, is typified on the one hand by the perversely dissappointing and vacant films featuring Jean-Paul Belmondo as a Rambeau-style (sic) hero-cop, and on the other by the big budget picaresque epics glorifying a practically nativist sense of French identity, especially in the films of Claude Berri (*Manon of Spring*, *Jean de Florette*, *Germinal*). This situation forms the backdrop for the specificity of *La Haine* as it was created in its historical moment. Funded by Canal + and La Sept Cinéma, and promoted by Jodie Foster, *La Haine* negotiated its way around substantial resistance, even to the point of rejecting public funding because of the conditions that would have been imposed.

Part of the importance of *La Haine*, thus, comes from the fact that it represents a part of French society that is marginal, and that in the 1990s was increasingly being excluded, by means of anti-immigrations laws, identity checks, and a white-washed version of French identity, from society. The film contains some extraordinary representations of the culture wars in France, such as the mixing of songs like "The Sound of Da Police" by KRS-1 with Edith Piaf singing "Je ne regrette rien," as the camera floats above the rooftops of the *banlieues*. The use of Bob Marley's "Burnin' and a Lootin'" too is significant; more than any other musician Marley has come to be identified with the struggle for postcolonial cultural revival.

In the *banlieues*, the figure of the gangster rapper has emerged as the inheritor of the symbolic role of icon of postcolonial popular identity. I see this identification as rooted in the search for examples in negotiating the complicated question of French identity, in which the equality before the law of all citizens regardless of origin is often severely compromised by the political and judicial system, and in which it is sometimes difficult for youths to find the image of themselves in cultural products. There has been a tendency to look to the United States as a model or alternative, partly because of its ideals as symbolized by notions of the melting pot, partly because of the history of protest for black civil liberties, and partly because of the attractiveness of the style and rhetoric of hip hop, which advertises images of black pride and disregard for prevailing pieties. These projections become badly dehistoricized in the cross-cultural comparisons to which they give rise. Instead of an image of American society in which racial inequality has continued to be so deeply entrenched as to mobilize protest, one is left with an image of the protest alone.

Ironically, however, in *La Haine* it is primarily Vinz, the Jewish-French protagonist, who identifies most strongly with the image of the gangster, while the African Hubert is very critical and Sayid prevails upon both of them to compromise. This again suggests a level of complexity denied by the popular references to the movie in the context of a monolithic representation of the *banlieues*. Vinz's identification with the gangster role is an interesting example of the symbolic inversions that can happen when cultural products and symbols are diffused by means of a capitalist system of exchange, in effect reversing the Marxian notion of alienation. Once separated from it original context, the product is rendered accessible for appropriation by the relatively privileged white American suburbanite like the French *"banlieusard,"* each isolated in their own way from the urban center; in both cases a perceived authenticity forms the metaphysical basis for a new imagined identity: the *banlieue*-gangster. Refracted in the shattered mirror of decentered subjectivity, the postcolonial "African" surviving in the concrete jungle becomes the personification of righteous otherness (and by association, pure truth) in an almost complete reversal of the mystification that motivated the previous century's search for the heart of darkness. At one point early in the movie, Kassovitz has Vinz looking at himself in the mirror pretending to draw his gun: "C'est à moi que tu parles, putain!" he repeats, "C'est à moi que tu parles?" [Are you talking to me, bitch?] Kassovitz's allusion to *Taxi Driver* is poignant. But who is the imagined other that Vinz is speaking to, and of which he becomes an alienated symbol? Himself. France. Culture.

The final scene of *La Haine* in which Hubert faces off with a police officer is finely realized. Just before the confrontation, a mural of Baudelaire watches over the heros, functioning as a darkly ironic counterpoint to the forthcoming scene, again opposing the public display of "high art," designed to perpetuate the ideals of French civilization, with the social reality of the *banlieues* as signified by the youths. Vinz finally surrenders the gun that he found during the previous day's rioting to Hubert, who throughout the film had been trying to convince Vinz of the futility of violence and the inauthenticity of his gangster posture. There is a false denouement; the conflict of the film seems to have come to a resolution. But as they walk off, the police arrive and begin harrassing Vinz and Sayid. Hubert watches from a short distance as one of the officers (an Arab) puts a gun to Vinz's head. The gun goes off. Hubert approaches as if in a trance. He points his gun at the police officer. The police officer raises his gun. The screen goes dark; a shot is heard. It is at this point that the anecdote of the fall is retold for the last time, but now in a different way: "C'est l'histoire d'une *societé* qui tombe d'une immeuble de cinquante étages." [It's the history of a *society* that falls from a fifty story building.]

I began this essay with the commonplace notion that social reality had to be distinguished from its representation in narrative form to analyze the way in which reality is constructed in the docu-fictional narrative form. I believe that there are some essential connections that one must look for in the historical context of contemporary France to do justice to *La Haine*, but the interpretation must also pay attention to the play of symbols and metaphors within the text itself. In contrast to what one would expect from newspaper articles and the surrounding cultural rhetoric, the film, probably as a consequence of attention to the problems of characterization rather than because of any polemical intent, reveals itself to be carefully structured so as to convey the idealist conception that structural oppositions like the ones between the police and the youth, official culture and subculture, world culture and French culture, Paris and the *banlieue*, fiction and reality, and inside and outside are arbitrary. At the same time, however, the film can be seen to affirm the materialist counter-interpretation: that in our experience of reality we are constantly forced by circumstances and by social structures to negotiate our way in a world in which division is an essential part, and taking sides can often be a simple function of where one happens to be standing.

WORKS CITED

Amar, Marianne & Milza, Pierre. *L'Immigration en France au Vingtième Siècle.* Armond Colin Éditeur: Paris, 1990.

Anderson, Benedict. *Imagined Communities*. Verso: New York, 1991.

Bachelard, Gaston. *The Poetics of Space*. Beacon Press: Boston, 1994.

Baudrillard, Jean. *Selected Writings*. Trans. Mark Poster. Stanford UP: Stanford, 1988.

Bedarida, Catherine. "Quand les territoires d'exclusion se transforment en lieux de création; Les expériences mêlant jeunes des banlieues et artistes confirmés se multiplient." *Monde* 18 Jan. 1996.

Begag, Azouz. "The 'Beurs,' Children of North-African Immigrants in France: The Issue of Integration. *Journal of Ethnic Studies* 18.1 (1990).

Billiez, Jacqueline. "Les Jeunes Issus de l'Immigration Algérienne et Espagnole à Grenoble: Quelques Aspects Sociolinguistiques." *International Journal of the Sociology of Language.* Sociolinquistics in France: Current Research in Urban Settings 54 (1985).

Bourdieu, Pierre. *Language & Symbolic Power*. Harvard UP: Cambridge, 1994.

Calvet, Louis-Jean. "Français et Urbanisation." *Le Français dans l'Espace Francophone: Description Linguistique et Sociolinguistique de la Francophonie.* Honoré Champion Éditeur: Paris, 1993.

Delboulbes, Marie-Therese. "Mathieu Kassovitz: 'Le Monde peut s'écrouler, ici tout continue.' *Agence France Presse* 26 May 1995.

Do the Right Thing. Directed by Spike Lee. 1988.(?)

Genin, Catherine. "Les Jeunes des cités ont inventé leur propre langage." *Monde* 2 Sep. 1995.

Gildea, Robert. *France Since 1945*. OUP: New York, 1996.

Gumbel, Andrew. "Pasqua Plays Race Card." *New Statesman & Society.* 18 Jun. 1993.

Hall, Peter A., Hayward, Jack, and Machin, Howard eds. *Developments in French Politics*. Macmillan: London, 1993.

Hargreaves, Alec G. *Immigration, 'Race' and Ethnicity in Contemporary France.* Routledge: London & New York, 1995.

———— "Writers of Magrebian Immigrant Origin in France: French, Francophone, Maghrebian, or Beur?" Eds. Ibnlfass & Hitchcott. *African Fracophone Writing*. Berg: Washington, D.C., 1996.

Hebdige, Dick. *Subculture: The Meaning of Style*. Routledge: New York, 1979.

James, Caryn. "Crime, Violence and Pessimism (Not in America)." *New York Times* 12 Oct. 1995: C20.

La haine. Directed by Mathieu Kassovitz. 1995.

Noiriel, Gérard. *The French Melting Pot: Immigration, Citizenship, & National Identity*. University of Minnesota Press, Minnesota, 1996.

Petitclerc, J.M. *La Banlieue de l'Espoir*. Éditions Don Bosco: Paris, 1995.

Philippe, Bernard. "Ile-de-France cumulant les handicaps sociaux et urbanistiques." *Monde* 21 Oct. 1994.

Quermonne, Jean-Louis, *Le Gouvernement de la France sous la cinquième république*. Dalloz: Paris, 1980.

Riding, Alan. "Rage of France's Minorities Burns Through in Film Genre." *New York Times* 27 July 1995.

Rosenblum, Mort. "'The Other France' is Peopled with Anger, Poverty and Despair." *Los Angeles Times.* 4 Aug. 1996: A1.

Sanders, Carol, ed. *French Today: Language in its Social Context*. Cambridge UP: 1993.

Silverman, Maxim. *Deconstructing the Nation: Immigration, Racism and Citizenship in Modern France*. Routledge: London & New York, 1992.

Solaar, Claude MC. *Qui Sème le Vent Récolte le Tempo*. Polydor: Paris, 1991.

————. *Prose combat*. Polydor: Paris, 1994.

Tribalat, Michèle. *De l'immigration à l'assimilation: enquête sur les populations d'origine étrangère en France*. Éditions la Découverte/INED: Paris, 1996.

Winters, Laura. " Boyz in the Banlieue: Mathieu Kassovitz Unleashes Hate." *Village Voice.* 9 Feb. 1996: 54.

Section 4

LITERARY CRITICISM

10

THE PROJECTIONIST
in Sylvain Bemba's *Rêves portatifs**

by Lydie Moudelino

Although it is not until after the 1960's that African cinema develops significantly as the artistic production of Africans, one can say that even during the colonial era some Africans were already participating in the cinematic experience.[1] They were not filmmakers, or cameramen, or screenwriters. Rather, they served as technicians, cashiers, and ushers, and all those assistants essential to the distribution in Africa of images produced by Europeans, the cultural outsiders.

In *Rêves portatifs*, (1979), the Congolese writer Sylvain Bemba imagines the misadventures of one of these movie "assistants" in a Central African country in the late 50's, through the character of a projectionist, Ignace Kambeya. Since 1940, Kambeya has been practicing the profession of projectionist at the Lumière theater, in his village. Literally speaking, his job consists of projecting images onto the screen in order to entertain an enthusisatic indigenous audience.[2] In the general context of the period when he makes his career, this function appears to be intimately linked to the colonial politics of France. It is not just images that he is transmitting thanks to his technical abilities, it is an entire *imaginaire* imported from Europe that he helps convey. Seen in this light, the projectionist, not unlike the European creators, producers, and distributors of film in Africa, acts as a conduit of the colonial *imaginaire*. In this, as shown in the following passage, the projectionist is comparable to an illusionist, a projector of *portable dreams* as suggested by the title of Bemba's novel. This is precisely how Kambeya likes to conceive of his role in the community:

> Ignored, despised, misunderstood in the city, Ignace would wait each day for this miraculous moment which allowed him to take his revenge. By the precision, the steadiness of his movements which animated the machines which would, in turn, give life to a prestigious world of sound, of colors, and of forms, Ignace equaled the prestige of the white master . . . Ignace controlled one of the thousand marvels brought by the Europeans. He had even begun

> believing that his hands made and unmade the life of man, that they distributed glory and rendered justice. He claimed the surging clamors of praise, aimed at the invincible protagonist on the screen, as his own, enchanter that he was. It seemed to him that these tumultuous manifestations, which shook the theater, were solely intended to recognize his know-how. (11)

In the movie theater, home of the "miracle maker" (9), typically three types of films dominate: the American western, the Indian melodrama, and the French comedy (of Fernandel). Common to these three genres is a conformity to semi-invariable scenarios which present, film after film, specific social and moral behaviors. From a structural point of view, this type of film is organized—as shown by Vladimir Propp with the fairy tale—according to a combination of limited sequences and motives, which have the effect of presenting a certain conception of life. Thus, adventure, love and comedy propose discourses on Good and Evil, on honor and duty, and on the victory of justice and of resistance over adversity, all of which, in their endless repetition, end up imposing on the viewers a manichean perception of the world. The criticisms of the impact of this type of film on all audiences are well-known. However, as film-maker and critic Paulin Vieyra suggests,

> The danger of these films could be greater in Africa than in the Western World . . . They create mental habits, completely opposed to what would be preferable to invent for the young nations in the midst of development . . . A certain genre of films has a dreamlike function here, essentially destined, it seems, to prepare the ground for all possible propaganda (242).

Among the disastrous effects of pre-independence cinema on the African public, the control of the *imaginaire* exercised by colonial authorities, through the monopoly of circuits of diffusion and of film productions, is of monumental significance. It is this process of acculturation, "colonizing the mind" that Sylvain Bemba calls into question in *Rêves portatifs*, where, with a plot centered on the career of a projectionist, he proposes a greater reflection not only on cinema, but on the conjunction between reality and illusion at the crucial turning point in African history represented by the symbolic date of January 1, 1960. The propensity to confuse reality and fiction, inherent in the media itself and exacerbated by the conditions of its emergence in Africa, constitutes, according to Vieyra, another danger of "imported" cinema:

> In the majority of cases, the audience finds itself faced with films which present themselves as images of truth and which do not grant the viewer any possibility of distinguishing between fiction and reality . . . Because he is totally outside of Western civilization and has no point of comparison, an African confronted with a vision of an European production is forced to accept as true, or for expression of reality, the image he is being shown. (301)

"We are talking," adds Vieyra, "about a mainstream audience."[3]

In this first critique of the "portable dream" which begins to take shape, two closely related effects of colonial cinema are called into question : on the one hand, the crucial role played by the media as an instrument of acculturation and of domination of the imagination, which is characteristic of the colonial project; on the other hand, the audience's lack of awareness of the film as aesthetic artifice.

As such, if one considers the contractual relationship established between the film and its audience, the space of the movie theater itself can be considered a playing field. In his *Les jeux et les hommes*, Roger Caillois identifies six formal characteristics of games. According to Caillois, game can essentially be defined as follows:

> A free activity: to which the player must not feel obligated lest the game lose its aspect of alluring and joyful entertainment; a separate activity: restricted to pre-determined and well-defined limits of space and time; an indistinct activity: the development of which must not be determined nor the result acquired beforehand, a certain inventive latitude must be left to the initiative of the players; an unproductive activity; a regulated activity: submitted to conventions which suspend the ordinary laws and which institute momentarily a new legislation, which is the only thing that counts; and/or a fictitious activity: accompanied by a specific awareness of secondary reality or by clear-cut non-reality in comparison to everyday life. (43)

In view of these characteristics, cinema, like reading, can effectively conceive of itself as a play activity: limited to the theater where the public renders itself of its own free will, ready to receive no other gratification than that of submitting itself, for a limited time, to a series of different laws from those of everyday life, and of which it has an awareness of the artificial nature. I insist on Caillois' criteria in order to analyze one of the central events in the evolution of Bemba's character which causes his downfall, and eventually his death.

After work, Ignace Kambeya leaves his projection booth to go to a working-class bar, where he finds himself involved in a fight. He gets punched. Hallucinating, he goes crazy and stabs his attacker to death. He is arrested for murder and will finish his life in prison while the rest of the country prepares itself to celebrate its independence on January 1, 1960.

The demise of the projectionist, and his definitive exclusion from the community, is provoked by what Caillois calls "contamination" between the separate universes of fiction and "reality." Caillois insists on the necessity of a strict separation of these spheres:

> [These characteristics] which place the play world in opposition to the real
> world, and which emphasize that the game is essentially an activity aside,
> indicate that all contamination with everyday life runs the risk of corrupting or
> ruining its very nature.

The game is contaminated by the real—so it must be suspended—
continues Caillois, when "the strict barrier which separates them . . . loses
its necessary clarity" (102). In Bemba's case, the demise of the
projectionist is triggered by a contamination altogether opposite to that
described by Caillois: It isn't because the real encroaches on the space of
the game, but because the law of the game feigns to apply to the real that
the boundaries are blurred. The deviation, in Ignace's case, consists of
losing an awareness of the real (hallucination) to the point of really
believing himself to be a western hero, and to actually behaving according
to the logic of the interiorized film in twenty years of career. "The offense
always called for immediate vengeance, according to the law of cinema"
constitutes the only justification that Ignace invokes (27). We mustn't
forget, as states one of the interrogating officers, that: "this man . . . has
seen at least 70,000 crimes, about an average of 10 attacks per film per
day, that we multiply by 20 years of career (58) . . . The transgression, or
passage from one system to another, makes him a criminal, whereas he
saw himself as an upholder of the law of the West.

The projectionist will die from having lost, according to the Caillois'
terms, the "specific consciousness of a secondary reality," of the fictive
quality of the play activity. Such a deviation is sanctioned by the exclusion
of the character from the two universes: Banished from the real world and
the projection booth, the fallen projectionist has no place other than his
prison cell, the space *par excellence* of the outlaw and of radical
marginality. Even in prison, the *imaginaire* of the film is of no recourse.
For example, we see him dream of a western scene in which he has become
the hero:

> Ignace leaves his hiding-place, dusts off his magnificent suit, readjusts an
> extravagantly colored tie, and with an air of satisfaction, examines his fingers
> full of gold rings . . .

However, the film scenario, confused with a dream, does not come to
the rescue of reality. Ignace the cowboy doesn't save Ignace, the prisoner.
In front of the irruption of the real, the film imagination loses all
effectiveness, and reveals itself essentially useless: "The door violently
opens and interrupts this beautiful daydream. Two police officers are there:
"Ignace, follow us" (98). After this irremediable "Ignace, follow us," the
hope that life be like a film, or that the logic of the film saves one's life, is
definitively lost. Furthermore, one realizes that not only cinema, but the

white master himself, abandons him. In fact, his last hope resides in the conviction that this symbolically named Mr. Gaulois, his "boss," will get him out of prison: "'We're right,' he thinks to himself, 'to work hard for the Whites. Just like the singers say in the city, the White is my father and my mother . . . If Mr. Gaulois is there, it's to get him out of this mess" (112). When the White man, ignoring the heartbreaking calls of his former employee, leaves without looking back, the politic of colonial paternalism also reveals itself as a practice of delusion. And so ends the reign of the projectionist, condemned forever more to be, in a new cabin, a mere solitary spectator of a scenario which develops in spite of him. No one will conduct any miracles for this "miracle maker."

As pointed out by numerous film historians in Africa, the history of film and that of colonization intersect remarkably. The end of the nineteenth-century witnessed the official invention of cinema in 1895 and the partition of the African continent into colonies following the Berlin conference. With Pierre Hafner, we see that the two events, one in the domain of arts and the other geopolitical, meet in that "on one side and on the other, it was all about limiting gaze and space, by the boundaries of States or the frame of the camera, this obscure room from which exits so many marvels and so many monsters, used to so many ends" (82). The twentieth-century would then open upon the triumph of the European machine, in the combined exploitation of the dark continent and the dark room.

In *Rêves portatifs*, Bemba takes up this coincidence, this time surrounding the symbolic date of January 1, 1960. In the novel, this date marks the official passage from colonial status to that of an independent state, and more metaphorically, from a state of lethargy to one of being awake. From an historical "coincidence,"[4] by which in the 1960's the decolonization and the creation of new nations in Africa is contemporaneous to the beginnings of African cinema, Bemba rewrites a synchronic history of the developments of film and independence.

In this relationship, the common problem of the limits between dream and reality serves to elaborate a discourse on the very conception of Independence in the imagination of the peoples. As such, the chapter entitled "The wedding night of African independence," demonstrates well to what extent independence is conceived and lived like a glorious unraveling of a film scenario:

> The event is awaited with great, unanimous fervor. One word— independence—has created this climate.

> In the country of palm trees, one prepares feverishly, notably in Inoco, the capital. Across the urban perimeter of the town, the authorities have set up collective radio listenings. Kilometers of cables weave a sonorous spider web around Inoco and erect its speakers on the public square. Each day, the Inoquoise population becomes an Ear destined to receive the official word. This will have prophetic accents; it will announce happiness on credit, wellness within reach of all, the unlimited distribution of liberty. (8)

Later, in the scene showing the arrival of the "independence train" to town, the rhythmic acceleration of the story, the evocation of sounds, the enthusiasm of the crowd echoes in a striking way the cowboy scene described at the beginning of the novel. Part-cowboy, part locomotive of the Far-West, "independence" seems to burst out of the screen with sound, speed, and images: "Lipanda is coming, Lipanda is here! Toot Toot Lipanda . . ." (136). The entire town resembles an immense film set. The town arenas, the chosen place for the festivities, are in the same process transformed into a movie theater of gigantic dimensions which gathers an enormous crowd:

> The twenty thousand people who were able to literally pack into this arena . . . go into a trance . . .
>
> At eleven-thirty, the stadium lights up like a marvel. The visual shock is such that twenty thousand mouths let out a prolonged cry of surprise. The violently lit steps shake with life, with chanting. Lipanda is going to be born, Lipanda is going to enter through the doors of the stadium. (137)

The nation is no longer chanting the name of a foreign hero, but that of its own hero, Lipanda. Lipanda, the first African hero, imposes himself on the screen and institutes with him a new series of laws and behaviors:

> Lipanda will come at midnight. He was only a vague and remote idea. In approaching, he became hope. Now that he is almost within voice's reach, the populations have personified him and have given him a masculine gender because he will be the equalizer of opportunity among all the Palmériens [the citizens of the new nation], the leveler of their dreams, the public distributor of liberty. (124)

With the arrival of "independence" (Lipanda), the colonized space of the movie theater explodes. Interestingly, the new hero that bursts out of the screen shares with the cowboy not only a dedication to justice, but his stereotypically male attributes. In order to become a national hero, "Independence" which is feminine in French, changes to masculine, suggesting that in the substitution of power figures that is taking place, only another male figure overrules the era of the "cowboy."

The function of the new spectacle which replaces the cinema of the colonial era is to bring together the crowd as a nation, to constitute it and sanction it as reality. The symbolic historical event marks a radical transformation of the indigenous peoples into actors and directors of the spectacle. In other words, they no longer accept imported scenarios, they have ceased to be colonized. They will live and write their own history, will project their own dreams. As the first president makes it clear in his opening speech, the beginning of the new era should be compared to the first page of a brand-new notebook:

> Our country, which is going to be independent will resemble the first blank page of your notebook on the first day of school. It's up to you to write in it, instructed by our example, by the experience of those who preceded you, what our country holds to be most pure, most noble, most prized. (118)

The metaphor of the blank notebook implies here that access to independence requires a total erasure of the colonial past. Interestingly, the choice of this particular metaphor undescores the challenges faced by the leaders of the new nation and raises a series of crucial questions. School— with writing and notebooks as instruments—was one of the most powerful, indeed successful colonial institution. Thus the very means to inscribe the new history (writing in the book) is itself a legacy of colonialism. In what language will that new book be written? The dream of a new beginning that unfolds reminds us of the fundamental question raised by V. Mudimbe in *The Invention of Africa*. When the urgency of a redefinition of African knowledge becomes clear, in what terms can African intellectuals or politicians articulate, invent or reclaim a specific gnosis? In Molefi Asante's terms, to what extent is it possible to "step outside one's history" in a "final emancipatory gesture"? (5). Whether it concerns the nation, or in metaphorical terms the page or the screen, what is expressed here at the symbolic date of January 1, 1960 is the dream of a reculturation process that relies on a radical rupture with the past, while simultaneously attempting to reclaim an "authenticity." As we know however, the page is never blank, it is always already marked and whatever one sets out to inscribe on it has to follow—if it is to be readable—the rules of the game.

Mbye Cham affirms, in his *African Experiences of Cinema*, that African film must be considered as a product of decolonization: "African-film is in a way a child of African political independence. It was born in the era of heady nationalism and nationalist and anti-colonial struggle" (1). The causality between independence and the development of African film is indisputable. However, Bemba proposes here an interesting reversal of Cham's statement, by which one must consider this time the extent to which Independence is a product of cinema. In other words, how Independence as an imaginary construction inscribed itself into History and the memory of the people. This new issue of "portable dream" can be approached in its relation to dynamics of game-playing, again with a reference to Caillois. In regard to the relationship between game and institution, Caillois notes:

> Every institution functions in part like a game, so that it also presents itself as a game that must be instituted, based on new principles, and which must have chased an outdated game. This new game responds to other needs, values other norms and legislations, demands other virtues and other aptitudes. From this point of view, a revolution appears as a change in the rules of the game. (137)

The substitution of one political system for another, just like that of one spectacle for another, refers to what Caillois calls a "change in the rules of the game." Although one game (the colonial rule) has been dismissed, the new structures implement another one, with its laws and codes of behavior (the postcolonial rule). For illustration, let's return to the projectionist who is rotting in prison. With the arrival of Independence, the projectionist as an agent of imported imagination necessarily becomes an antiquated character. His era belongs from now on to a bygone past, to an old game driven away by new principles and new heroes. Neither him, nor the imagination that he relays, has a place in the nation (hence, the culture) which is taking shape.

It is not so much for having broken the law than for having been an accomplice to the colonizer that the projectionist is expulsed. As a criminal, he should have benefited from the general amnesty granted during Independence. In fact, all the prisoners leave their cells, except Ignace. The only prisoner in a free nation, Ignace is transformed into a scapegoat of an otherwise peaceful celebration. Ignace's exclusion, ultimately linked to the only violent act of the interregnum, thus symbolizes the refusal of illusion, the end of acculturation, the death of the colonized submitted to the laws of the colonizer's imagination.

The position of the projectionist as a scapegoat is explained then by the ambiguity of his position during the colonial era. On one level, Ignace's trial condemns the effects of cinema on the accused and on the public: "Ignace is a projectionist. The police cannot remain indifferent to the devastation caused by the media where social psychology is concerned" (58). If his profession, in particular, is called into question, on a more general level, his relation to a specific community is equally invoked. Thus, Bemba inscribes the individual history of the character into the collective history of colonization. At the beginning of the novel, Bemba distinguishes between two different groups of people: on one hand, the men of the plain and on the other, the men of the plateau. He opposes them according to their stance on colonialism. The projectionist belongs to the men of the plain, a group historically associated with the colonial project:

> Dedicated to their work, they rapidly adapted to the culture of the colonizer and constitute the majority of administrative assistants . . . They take pride in the fact that the Europeans came first to them, multiplying evangelical missions, commercial outlets and mulatto children before conquering the rest of the country. (8)

Ignace's filiation confirms what Bemba presents as an atavism of the "men of the the plain": His father was "one of the first automobile drivers of the country. The chauffeur was then considered as the closest friend of the White Man" (10). In this way, Ignace continues the function of his father and of his community in being, for twenty years, "the only projectionist of the Gaulois and son society" (10), that is to say, in being of service to the colonization of minds, symbolized by the patronymic of the owner. It is especially in this way that the end of his career, his demise, should also announce the end of the colonized.

Progressively, beyond the spectacle of the official celebration, "Independence" also reveals itself as a "portable dream," as one can see in the description of the political climate which reigns in the years following Independence. The first president, especially, represents the very type of idealist, blinded by the socio-political realities and is therefore useless. The result: "Two years after Independence, the collapse of institutions and moral values—backbone for any nation—is general" (173). The "nation" thus has no effective reality. One would believe, remarks the president, that one is reading "one of the tales from the Arabian Nights" (172). Later, during the president's fall, the unreal—cinema—takes its place again in the post colony in the transition to dictatorship. Instituting in this an entire literature centered on the figure of the dictator (Sony Labou Tansi, Henri Lopes, Thierno Monenembo) Bemba denounces in the second part of his story the reign of the autocrat as a "grotesque production" of a system which poses itself as real, through demagogic discourse, propaganda, and embellished lies. The post colony, once again, became the scene of a huge masquerade of legitimacy, institutes a rigged universe, governed above all else by a minister of the press and a new projectionist (184) at the service of the party which cuts across the country on board its cine-bus diffusing "authentic" documentaries.

In conclusion, I would like to refer back to a scene located in the middle of the novel, which seems to contain the whole issue of dreaming as Bemba sees it in the historical context of approaching Independence. The scene takes place in the prison where Ignace has just been brought, just before the amnesty which would liberate all the other prisoners. The projectionist engages his neighbor, a political prisoner and former journalist of the opposition, in conversation. "I killed a man" Ignace declares to his cell mate. The latter responds: "I killed a dream." And he explains:

> The men in power said that Independence would bring us everything . . . I compared the actual leaders to charlatans who pretend that life can imitate cinema where everything happens in the blink of an eye, whereas only cinema can imitate life, in its own way, by short cuts which don't exist in reality. (54)

The former projectionist and the former journalist are both condemned for having, in the eyes of the new government, committed a crime: One for having been of service to the ideology of the colonizer, the other for having criticized the discourses of Independence. One, then, for having projected "bad dreams," the other for not adhering to the national dream. Their common presence in the prison cell begs comparison. As shown earlier, the projectionist is singled out as a scapegoat of the symbolic liquidation of the colonial past. Even though a real act serves to project historical and political guilt onto him, he is no less legally a criminal. Like Meursault in Camus' *L'Etranger*, whatever the collective responsibility may be, the fact remains that he killed a man. The rebellious journalist, on the other hand, did not commit a crime in the legal sense of the term. Who is more guilty? Who is more a victim? He who "played the other's game" in his long career of illusionist of the colonial system, or he who denounces the dream of Independence as illusion? In Caillois' terms, Cassius the journalist would be considered a "game wrecker":

> He who breaks the spell, he who brutally refuses to acquiesce to the proposed illusion, who reminds the boy that he is not a real detective, a real pirate, a real horse, a real submarine, or the little girl that she is not rocking a real infant or that she is not serving a real meal to real ladies on her miniature dishes. (41)

In the meeting between the "dream supplier" and the "dream wrecker," Bemba seems to favor the latter. First of all, because he, the journalist, maintains an obvious resemblance with the writer. And then, because Cassius, unlike the naive Ignace, is portrayed as a conscious being, who reflects on the condition of modern Africa, and who especially takes his turn at projecting hope at the end of the novel. However the final dream projected in the novel, as the interrogative form suggests, is devoid of both idealism and personal ambition:

> It's the awakening, he dreams, before the end of dictatorship. "Is it finally the revenge of the people? Yesterday cuckolded by dream merchants, placed in the impediment of creating children in Africa. (206)

These last words which reintroduce hope into the novel, after having made of the projectionist a martyr of History, summarize the issue of the "portable dream" which Bemba develops all along his novel, which is that of the cyclical but necessary and inevitable return of the dream.[5] The final image is that of an Africa deceived by the succession of "nightmare projectors." It is not the dream itself which is called into question here, but rather the "portable" dream, the sterile "ready-to-dream" put to the use of specific political projects (of charlatans), aiming to dominate the minds and the imaginations instead of inciting them to a productive creativity of culture (of liberty).

NOTES

[*]I would like to express my sincere thanks to Renée K. Gosson for the translation of this article from French.

1. As noted by Paulin Vieyra, "we must date the existence of African film back to 1924," date of the short film *La Fille de Carthage* by Tunisian filmmaker Chemana Chikly. However, he goes on to say that "African film, born in 1924, experiences a rebirth between 1953 and 1957, and begins to develop after the independence of African countries." I will cite then the 1960s as the period when African film production begins to be recognized (notably thanks to the world festival of Black arts in Dakar (1966) and to the Pan African cultural festival of Algiers in 1969 (Vieyra 17-19). The 1960s would also see the launching of the *Days of Carthage* in 1966 and the creation of FESPACO in 1969.

2. During the colonial era, there were circuits of diffusion (choice of films, projection rooms) reserved for the indigenous audience.

3. These remarks by Vieyra concern the 1970s, but I hold them all the more relevant for the novel's audience, in the 1950s-1960s.

4. The quotation marks refer to what I consider the "coincidence" in the sense of simultaneity, which does not deny the causality between the two events or developments.

5. which does not mean that Bemba refuses the place either of the dream or of cinema as a genre in civil life. Bemba does not at all call into question the real artists that are the African filmmakers.

WORKS CITED

Molefi Asante. *Kemet, Afrocentricity and Knowledge*. Trenton, NJ : Africa World Press, 1990.

Imruh Bakari and Mbye B. Cham (ed). *African Experiences of Cinema*. British Film Institute, 1996.

Sylvain Bemba. *Rêves portatifs*. Paris: Nouvelles Editions Africaines, 1979.

Roger Caillois. *Les Jeux et les hommes*. Paris: Gallimard, 1958.

Pierre Hafner. "Stratégies du cinéma mobile: une note pour une histoire parallèle du cinéma et de l'Afrique." In *L'Afrique et le centennaire du cinéma*. Fepaci. Paris: Présence Africaine, 1995.

Paulin Soumanou Vieyra. *Le cinéma africain. Des origines à 1973*. Paris: Présence africaine, 1975.

11

Sycorax Video Style: Kamau Brathwaite's Middle Passages

by Linda Lizut Helstern

In a 1974 essay, Kamau Brathwaite considered those voices which had been submerged by white European voices in the creation of New World culture and history. Brathwaite entitled the essay "Timehri," a Warraou Indian term he learned from the Guyanese painter Aubrey Williams—the name for the rock paintings, the petroglyphs, made by the Warraou ancestors. For Aubrey Williams, they had been a visual inspiration. For Brathwaite, they were hints of an all-but-silenced worldview: "glimpses of a language, glitters of a vision of the world, scattered utterals of a remote Gestalt; but still there, near, potentially communicative" (40). Nearly twenty years later, the poet whose work has so often focused on bringing a submerged African identity to black Caribbean consciousness would return to this submerged Amerindian element. *Middle Passages*, published in the Columbus quincentennial year 1992, pays homage to indigenous America, not by attempting to colonize its worldview but by incorporating potentially communicative glyphs into revisions of poems to render the New World on its own terms. Brathwaite extends the visual element in his work with a type face of his own design, which he has named Sycorax Video Style. *Middle Passages* represents Brathwaite's first use of this face, which has become the signature of his most recent work.

His choice of name positions this type face—and all of Brathwaite's subsequent work—at the intersection of tradition and high technology. In his essays, Brathwaite frequently applies the paradigm from Shakespeare's *Tempest* to discussions of Caribbean identity. For him, Sycorax, the African mother superceded by Prospero, holds the key to Caribbean cultural authenticity, which begins in language (Torres-Saillant 705). If vestiges of the African mother tongue survive in the Caribbean spoken vernacular, these creolized languages have never achieved legitimacy in print intended for any reading audience beyond the islands (and only a very limited use, mainly in newspaper humor columns, in print media there). As a premier performance poet, Brathwaite is keenly aware that contemporary poetry faces just the opposite problem: its essential orality submerged in print, poetry has lost its popular audience. Brathwaite sees Sycorax Video Style as a means of reconnecting the oral and the visual, high culture and mass culture through typographic design, finding justification for his project in traditional cultures. He notes, "I think that oral traditions do have a very strong visual aspect. In the African tradition, they use sculpture. Really, what I'm trying to do is create word sculptures on the page, but word-song for the ear" (Rigby 708). Brathwaite's recognition of the potential of graphic design began with his use of the computer, which allowed him to play with images as he has played with words, engaging in a video game with high cultural dimensions. His experiment finds an analog in twentieth century cinema, where audio-visual technologies have produced art with mass audience appeal.

With a single exception, the poems in *Middle Passages* are recycled from Brathwaite's previous publications. Most revisions focus on the visual impact rather than the content of the poems. Brathwaite may center the lines of a poem or set them flush right instead of flush left. It is Brathwaite's sparing use of the pictographic strategy that suggests its importance to *Middle Passages*. Aside from their title pages, only five of the book's fourteen poems venture into the realm of visual poetry. Despite variations in the reader face from poem to poem, the volume looks fairly standard. Of the five poems that incorporate specialized typographic elements, "Duke" and "How Europe underdeveloped Africa" use them to emphasize key phrases—to orchestrate the reading of the poem. Larger equals louder. Not only does Brathwaite employ typography for emotional emphasis as it is used in personal notes and letters, he also uses it to set the scene through visual allusions to signage—a crisply institutional public restroom sign in the former poem and a hand-lettered protest march sign in the latter. Oversize type inevitably slows the reader down: the sudden shift from reader face to display face emulates a cinematic jump cut from a long- or medium-range shot to a closeup, as in "Duke," where it freezes the eye meeting "SUPER/ NOVA HEADLIGHTS" head on or sustains a lingering focus on featured blues singer "IVIE ANDERSONNNG" (23, 25).

"Colombe" and "Letter Sycora X" achieve visual continuity through the repetition of one specialized typographic element, in each case a single letter, but the reader, like the film viewer, brings more information to the image with each repetition. The letters given graphic prominence seem at first glance purely decorative, in keeping with the curious page ornament in the middle of "Flute(s)." In fact, these letters and the ornament are glyphs encoding Mesoamerican cosmology into *Middle Passages*. It is no accident that the capital a's in the title typography suggest pyramids with their dual African-Mesoamerican identity. If Brathwaite sees the pyramids as the visual underpinning of the "strong oral tradition" of Egypt, the glyph is also intimately tied to Aztec and Mayan architecture (Rigby 708). In these cultures, scribes worked with equal facility on paper and in stone (Dennis Tedlock 27).

"Colombe," the second poem of *Middle Passages*, offers a deceptively simple glyph to start with. (See Plate 1.) Recognizing the initial c as a coiling snake, however, underscores

Plate 1. C, "Colombe."

hidden levels of meaning in the poem, levels difficult to access without this visual clue. The c stands alone, an ominous presence centered above each of the poem's three sections. It is not until the conclusion of the second section, when Brathwaite's lines "tipped black boot in my belly. the/ whips uncurled desire?" evoke the slave master's infamous blacksnake that the ominous hint takes on a concrete association (11). When in the third section of the poem, Brathwaite describes a paradise complete with "bearded fig trees," the snake becomes the serpent of paradise, the biblical agent who with the temptation of Eve wrenched historic linear time from eternity. At the same time, the repetition suggests the Mesoamerican notion of the repetition of time in cyclically recurring patterns, and one comes to the sudden realization that "Colombe" is nothing less than a reenactment of biblical creation, which has begun with Columbus, like God, moving over the surface of the waters. Light is divided from darkness, and land from water. Consciousness is divided as well. Limited human consciousness is set against omniscience with its knowledge of all time and all action. The latter understands the necessary consequence of the knowledge of evil. The former does not. Yet the paradise that Adam/Columbus is about to enter seems to him already inhabited, potentially threatening: he is sure he hears "soft voices mocking in the leaves" (11). Is this paranoia, intuition, or memory? Is there any rational meaning in the act of discovering the New World? Brathwaite's omniscient narrator frames the question in Columbus's mind: is this, in fact, "Dis/ covery? or a return to terrors/ he had sailed from. known before?"

A break in the form of the poem at once emphasizes Columbus's uncertain pause and gives the reader an opportunity to weigh the possiblity of historic repetition against the prevailing notion of a new beginning in a land previously unknown. It is, of course, a return, though Columbus moves ahead according to accepted New Testament notions of linear, apocalyptic time—time which must be redeemed, to use a favorite phrase of the Protestant Reformation. Is it a curious accident of history that within a year after Luther had posted his Theses on the door of Wittenburg Cathedral, Cortez would conquer the Aztec empire, effectively submerging the world's most astronomically accurate and profound expression of sacred cyclical time beneath its Western European linear construct? In each new paradise, of course, Europeans cast the native peoples in the role of the Satanic snake, the voice Columbus thinks he hears in the trees. With instinctive wariness, the crabs retreat from the aggressive intruder, suggesting that the real threat to paradise comes from the outside.

Brathwaite's circling snake encodes not only the biblical serpent but also the Mesoamerican calendar. (See Plate 2.) The first poem of *Middle Passages* contains an explicit reference to this calendar: "Word Making Man" is dedicated to the politically committed Cuban poet Nicolas Guillén and celebrates a shared faith in the power of the word.

Plate 2. Aztec Calendar Stone.

In the poem Guillén himself becomes the snake "circling circling circling renewing yr cycle of certainty" (3). The transformation occurs as a consequence of the politically motivated murder of the poet's father, himself a politically committed writer, though a journalist rather than a poet. Through his life, Guillén would repeatedly bear witness in his work to a seemingly endless cycle of political murders of friends and acquaintances. Brathwaite's shorthand permits a dual reading of yr as both your and year as he invokes the greatest image of renewal in the New World, the Aztec calendar stone, ringed by two snakes symbolic of time (Alarcón). Coded into this representation of the cosmos are the formulas which permitted Mesoamerican astronomer/priests to calculate with extraordiary precision the cyclic recurrence of astronomical phenomena millions of years into the past and the future (Tompkins 299). Great rituals marked the end of one cycle and the beginning of another, with great significance attached to the simultaneous ending/beginning of two or more cycles. In the case of the two most commonly used time cycles, the 365-day solar year and the 260-day divinatory year, this occurred every fifty-two years. The entire cycle would then repeat itself (Schele and Miller 17).

In his use of Spanish spellings for such key words as Jamaica and Shango, rendered as Xaymaca and Xangô, Brathwaite encodes New World history into "Word Making Man" in yet another way. The letter x was the convention adopted by the Spanish for rendering the sh sound in Amerindian languages, a sound which did not occur in Spanish (Schele and Miller 7). Columbus set foot on Jamaica in 1594, and the island was claimed by Spain for more than fifty years before it was ceded to England. Xaymaca was the Spanish alphabetic rendering of the Arawak name for the island, a word meaning "land of springs" (Davis 9). Xangô, of course, is of African origin. The letter x forges a commonality of experience between tribal peoples on two continents who came under European domination. Today in the Caribbean, their languages and identities survive in creolized forms. (It should be mentioned that Brathwaite's history scholarship has centered on the creolization process. He has authored such works as *The Development of Creole Society in Jamaica 1770-1820* and "Caliban, Ariel, and Unprospero in the Conflict of Creolization: A Study of the Slave Revolt in Jamaica in 1831-32.") When the x becomes a symbolic bond between the two poets as "Word Making Man" draws to its conclusion, the power of Xangô manifests itself through a creolized chant, a play on words which transforms no to yes, and bad to well, incorporating not only Spanish and English but Oriental pigeon English as well. No longer separated but unified by sound, the sound of the Caribbean Sea, black Caribbeans finally have the power and the words to claim the land "& know at last at last it is our home" (7). Posessing this, they possess nothing less than the cosmos "'w/ the vast splendour of the sunshine & the sunflower & the stars'" (7).

Having established a pattern of references and allusions to snakes in the book's first two poems, it is clearly no accident that Brathwaite prefaces the title of the third poem "Noom" with Damballa, the name of the powerful snake loa of vodun. Damballa, "as the source of the water that bubbles to the earth in springs," is nothing less than "the source of life itself"—life being synonomous with movement (Dayan 77). This is an invocation of extraordinary power for a poet who makes his home in the land of springs. The name is only a trace in Brathwaite's book, however: Damballa is not mentioned in any subsequent poem. Brathwaite seems to invoke Damballa here as an African survivor of the Middle

Passage, a spirit stronger than noom, a neologism which Brathwaite has glossed as "the sound of noon; the angelus of doom" and as "fatal noon" (*Sun Poem* 100 note; *X/Self* 127 note). "Noom" directly confronts the destruction of African tribal culture, offering with bitter sarcasm a "recipe" that will ensure its death without jeopardizing the conqueror. Ignoring indigenous language is a key step. Killing the priests of the traditional religions is even more important. Every vestige of their being must be eradicated. Their torture must continue even in death. This, the narrator suggests, can be accomplished by killing them on the high seas and dumping their bodies overboard into the shark-infested waters. The poem's great unstated irony, of course, is that the undersea route is the most direct route the spirit can take back to Africa.

Brathwaite's prescription is perfectly recognizable to all of the tribal peoples of the Americas: "teach them spanglish// preach them rum" (16). While "Noom" does not directly address the enslavement of Amerindians or the recurring pattern of atrocities against them, Brathwaite suggests a Native presence by embedding the tribal names navajo and aztec in his text. Even when the context is explicitly African and the use of the word totally unrelated to its meaning as a tribal designator, merely speaking the word aztec betokens an absent Amerindian presence. Interestingly, Brathwaite deleted the word injuns from the poem in the version published in *Middle Passages*, perhaps in recognition of the altered language sensitivity of readers since its first publication. In its place, he substituted engines, a near-homophone. In fact, the change is consistent with the pictographic strategy of the volume; engines provides a tantalizing glimpse of an underlying subliminal meaning, like the *timehri* which individuals outside Warraou culture are not privileged to understand.

Brathwaite follows his poem about cultural death with a poem of resurrection, and he places this resurrection in a specifically New World context, indeed, in a watery New World context. Through the miraculous agency of his keyboard music, Duke Ellington's aged alligator hands, like the Mesoamerican Calendar Round, turn young. Norman Weinstein reads the alligator as an allusion to the ancient Egyptian god renowned for his wisdom (718). While the identities of the alligator and the crocodile are often conflated, as Weinstein has done, it is significant that the crocodile is native to both Africa and the Americas. The alligator, like jazz, is strictly a New World animal. Brathwaite continues the New World music theme in the following poem "Flute(s)." The indigenous instruments of Africa, notably the drum, played a key role in Brathwaite's early trilogy *The Arrivants*. In *Middle Passages*, he assigns a similar role to the flute, which in contemporary film and television sound tracks has become the popular musical signature of Native America. The melody of the flute is counterpointed against the ominous drumbeat of "Noom." Its music is the music of light, the music of life—"the bright of sound," to use Brathwaite's own words (33). On a page by itself between the two pages of the poem floats a symbol that seems to be a randomly placed page ornament. (See Plate 3.) It is, in fact, a

Plate 3. Page Ornament, "Flute(s)."

Mesoamerican glyph of enormous significance, called the Cross of Quetzalcoatl by Laurette Séjourné in her landmark study *Burning Water*. (See Plate 4.) Séjourné cites the Codex

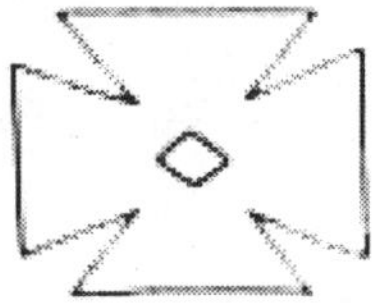

Plate 4. Cross of Quetzalcoatl.

Borbonicus as the source for the glyph she reproduces. There it appears in the context of the New Fire Ceremony, the ritual which marked the end of one fifty-two year Calendar Round and the beginning of the next. The extinction and rekindling of every fire in Mesoamerica symbolized the rebirth, the renewal of time itself (96).

The importance of rekindling the fire assumes an astronomical dimension in terms of the Venus cycle. Venus is the heavenly body specifically identified with Quetzalcoatl. In Mayan myth, Venus as the evening star originates as a fragment of the sun torn off before the sun's decline. It disappears from the west to reappear in the east ahead of the sun, the spark that rekindles the sun to blazing glory and is ultimately subsumed in its reunion with the father creator (Séjourné 58-59). Quetzalcoatl, in the context of the creation, performs an analogous function, saving the world from utter extinction. After the Fourth World/Fourth Sun is destroyed by a great flood, Quetzalcoatl journeys to the underworld and tricks the Lords of Death to win possession of human bones which he brings to life through the sacrifice of his own blood. He thereby brings the Fifth World into being. This world, our world, is symbolized by the glyph ollin, meaning movement in Nahuatl. In the simplest terms, it can be described as the letter x. A number of variants of this glyph are reproduced in Burning Water immediately following the Cross of Quetzalcoatl (Séjourné 96-97). (See Plate 5.)

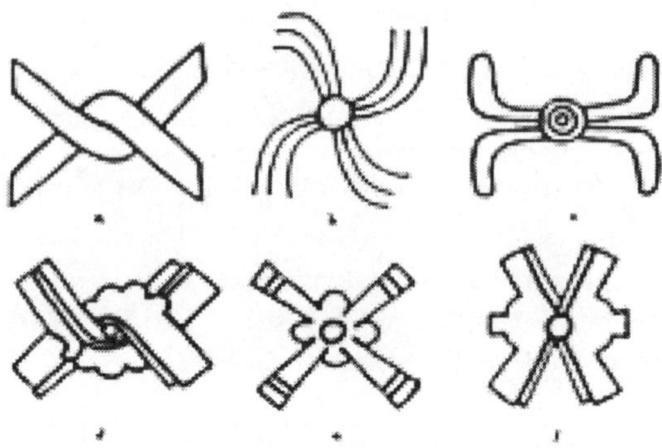

Plate 5. Ollin (Séjourné 97).

The form of the glyph renders visible the balance of power among the four elements which must be maintained for the duration of the Fifth World. Each pair of opposing elements, fire and water, earth and air, is represented by an arm of the x. The point where they meet, the centerpoint of the x, signifies the harmonious transfer of power from one to the next. Life exists in the context of the harmony of opposites in continuous motion.

It is, therefore, no accident that the third glyph Brathwaite plants in the text of *Middle Passages* is a x whose arms are snakes. (See Plate 6.) There could be no more appropriate

Plate 6. X, "Letter Sycora X."

identity for a creolized Caliban than this x of "Letter Sycora X". Here not elements but origins, diametrically opposed world views, are harmonized. The glyph suggests an evolution in Brathwaite's thinking. In her review of *X/Self*, where this poem first appeared under the title "X/Self's Xth Letters from the Thirteen Provinces," Joan Dayan observed that Brathwaite had borrowed this signature identity from Césaire. In *Une Tempete* when Caliban is given the opportunity to choose a new identity, he chooses the name X "to represent his missing past: 'Every time you call me, I am reminded that you've stolen everything from me: even my identity!'" (506). Brathwaite's glyph suggests that while the Caribbean identity remains an unknown quantity, it is a positive rather than a negative quantity. In the earlier version of the poem, the X, the traditional symbol for the unknown quantity in algebraic equations, looked appropriately mathematical, appropriately anonymous. That which had been excised could in no way be identified or replaced.

Brathwaite's glyph hints first of all at what is missing: x is the final letter of Sycorax. Brathwaite here endows Caliban's mother with a specifically African identity, that of "forest Nzinga." To restore the African element of Caribbean identity, for Brathwaite, is a positive step toward the restoration of a cosmos with a spiritual as well as a physical dimension, a cosmos that includes Sycorax, "the submerged feature of Shakespeare's play that we are very much involved with in the Caribbean" ("Caliban's Guarden" 166). She embodies the African component which Brathwaite has worked so hard to restore to Caribbean consciousness through his poetry, essays, and historical scholarship. To call Sycorax Nzinga is to invoke the name of the great seventeenth century queen who, for four decades, led her own armies and as a baptized Christian, forged critical alliances with the Portuguese and the Dutch to make her kingdom the most powerful in central Africa (Broadhead). Sycorax is no longer simply the white man's anti-Christian witch. Indeed, in Euro-American symbology, the Greek letter chi, our x, has traditionally represented Christ, finding its most common contemporary use in the shortened form Xmas. Just as traditional African and Amerindian religions found expression in the Christian practices of their conquerors, Brathwaite's X simultaneously encodes both Christianity and non-Christian religions in a harmony of opposites. It represents the true creole identity.

This change to a positive identity is nothing less than a change of historical perspective that Brathwaite also encodes in his poetic text through his careful choice of words and phrases, specifically Xerxes and Anglo Saxon Chronicles, featuring the letter x. Xerxes, which X substitutes for herpes, is far more than a malapropism. Beyond the coded reference to the European diseases which devastated the native population of the Caribbean within thirty years after Columbus's landing, Xerxes stands as an important historical reference point. Xerxes was the rebel Persian who was never given his due by the Greeks. He was, in fact, defeated in the Battle of Salamis, but not before he had burned Athens to the ground, permanently altering the course of Athenian history. In the wake of Xerxes, democracy became tyranny. What Brathwaite's X wants to write on his computer is something entirely his own, no mere repetitions of the social science strategies which before have always spoken for him. These strategies go back as far as written history itself, in the English-speaking world to the Anglo Saxon Chronicles. Even a dialectical response to Euro-American civilization is insufficient for X. As he cautions, "for not one a we shd response if prospero get/ curse/ wid im own curser" (107).

The first step in rewriting history is reclaiming one's own language, as Brathwaite suggests by rendering "Letter Sycora X" in the creolized Caribbean English which he calls nation language in his theoretical writings. Although Brathwaite has long championed nation language poets from Miss Lou to the young dub poets who emerged in Jamaica in the late seventies, on the few previous occasions when he has used nation language in his own work, Brathwaite has always used it in the context of speech. In adopting the epistolary form, Brathwaite here effects a brilliant synthesis of speech and written language. The poem is, in fact, a dramatic monologue on the supreme irony of X's discovery that he can write—and not in ink but in light (precisely as the biblical God rendered his word in light). The identity X discovers in the act of writing to his mother is the identity of the language "X/ pert" in the tradition of Moses and Aaron, the first priests of the biblical gods. The emblem of their priesthood was, in fact, two entwined serpents. With the aid of the high technology he has appropriated from Euro-America, X finally recoups all of his mother's powers. He is, indeed, a chip off the old block. A nobody has become truly a somebody.

Brathwaite offers a subtle clue to his Mesoamerican subtext when he uses the metaphor of stone carving for writing on the computer, "chipp/in dis poem onta dis tab./ let," as he describes it (115). Mesoamerican architects, sculptors, and scribes (who worked in both paper and stone) consciously exploited the effects of light and shadow in their work, creating friezes and sculptures that could virtually bring stone to life. Even today, equinoxes draw hundreds upon hundreds of visitors to Chichén Itzá to witness the miraculous movement between heaven and earth of the snakes at the four corners of the Castillo, popularly known as the Pyramid of Quetzalcoatl. The movement is created by the shadows cast by the sun when it reaches a particular angle. The s of Brathwaite's computer-designed type face Sycorax Video Style suggests precisely this phenomenon: it is a fluid rendering of his pyramid a. (See Plate 7.) An analysis of all of the various elements of the letters ties them to Mesoamerica. There

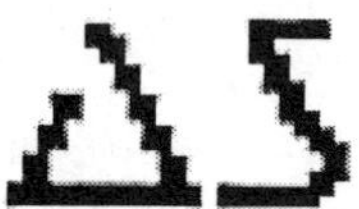

Plate 7. A, S: Sycorax Video Style.

are two primary elements, the Cross of Quetzalcoatl, from which Brathwaite evolves at least thirteen upper- and lower-case letters, typically through a reversal of the figure/ground relationship, and the seven-step pyramid, which is the basis of another nine letters. A snake glyph manifests itself in the c, the x, and the s, and in certain serifs recognizable as rattlesnake tails. (See Plate 8). A more abstract, almost rectangular, Mesoamerican snake glyph, is

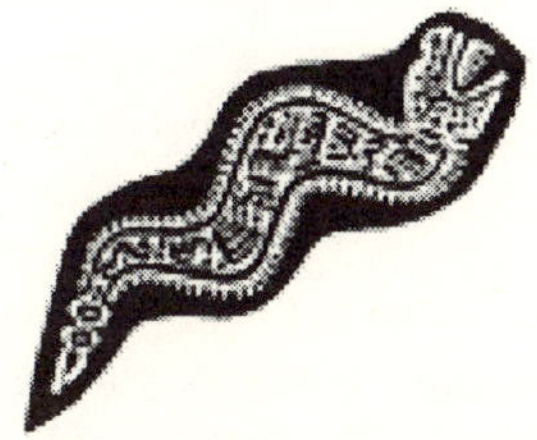

Plate 8. Aztec Snake Glyph.

refined into the capital letters e, m, and n. (See Plates 9 and 10.) The m and n simultaneously suggest the posts and lintels, which, inscribed with hieroglyphs, form the basis of Mesoamerican building systems and historical records. Even the simplest columnar

Glyph Plate 9. Aztec Snake.

Plate 10. E, M, N: Sycorax Video Style.

elements in Brathwaite's alphabet (the capital i, for example) incorporate pyramid-shaped "bases" and "capitals". (See Plate 11.)

I

Plate 11. I, Sycorax Video Style.

It is, perhaps, not out of line to suggest that there is also a very personal meaning encoded in Brathwaite's glyphs. Early in his marriage, Brathwaite nicknamed his wife Doris, a mixedblood Warraou from Guyana, Zea Mexican in honor of her Amerindian heritage (Walmsley 747). Accepting the Neustadt

International Prize in 1994, Brathwaite called her his "twin and opposite" when introducing his poem "Computer Legba." While his title suggests the role the computer has come to play in Brathwaite's life since his wife's death, a gateway to the world of the spirit, his epithet may be read as an allusion to Quetzalcoatl, often referred to as Precious Twin, particularly in light of the fact that Brathwaite here spoke of his "postmodern Sycorax video-style poetry" as "a kind of New Life poetry" (Brathwaite, "Newstead" 658). Doris Brathwaite's computer expertise predated the trend to personal computing, and her computer stood near her bedside throughout her terminal illness, when she lived in the hope of teaching her husband how to use it (Brathwaite, Zea 33). Kamau Brathwaite's first experiments with computer typography date from 1986, the year of her death, continuing for more than a decade when Brathwaite has carried within himself a keen personal sense of the absence of the Amerindian in the Caribbean.

It seems only appropriate to end this discussion by returning to the beginning of *Middle Passages*, specifically to the table of contents page where one significant glyph remains unidentified. (See Plate 12.) The double scroll Brathwaite uses here is a frequently used

Plate 12. Page Ornament, Table of Contents,
Middle Passages.

Mesoamerican glyph, often signifying a sacrificial offering in a tangible form. (See Plate 13.)

Plate 13. Mesoamerican Sacrifice Glyph Incorporated into Graphic Representation of Sacrifice (Campbell 160).

Depending on the context, the double scroll may represent the smoke offered through burning incense, the breath offered through music or poetry, or the flowing blood of blood sacrifice (Schele and Miller 43). Rising as it does above the titles of all of the poems in the book, this double scroll suggests that Brathwaite has dedicated his book as a sacred offering, hoping, in a tradition both African and Mesoamerican, to materialize the world of the spirit.

NOTE

I wish to express my thanks to those at Southern Illinois University at Carbondale whose support enabled me to present this paper at the 1997 conference of the African Literature Association: the Office of the Vice Chancellor for Academic Affairs and Provost, the Office of the Dean of the College of Liberal Arts, the Association of English Graduate Students and Instructors, and Professor Clarisse Zimra.

WORKS CITED

Alarcón, Francisco X. Personal interview. 21 July 1994.

Brathwaite, (Edward) Kamau. "Caliban's Guarden." *Wasafiri* 16 (Autumn 1992): 2-6.

———. *Middle Passages*. New York: New Directions, 1993.

———. "Newstead to Neustadt." *World Literature Today* 68.4 (Autumn 1994): 654-60.

———. *Sun Poem*. Oxford: Oxford U P, 1982.

———. "Timehri." *Is Massa Day Dead?* Ed. Orde Coombs. New York: Anchor, 1974.

———. *X/Self.* Oxford: Oxford U P, 1987.

———. *The Zea Mexican Diary*. Madison: U of Wisconsin P, 1993.

Broadhead, Susan H. "Njinga." *Historical Dictionary of Angola*. Metuchen, NJ: Scarecrow, 1992.

Davis, Stephen. *Reggae Bloodlines: In Search of the History and Culture of Jamaica*. New York: Anchor, 1977.

Dayan, Joan. "The Beat and the Bawdy." *The Nation* 9 April 1988: 504-507.

———, trans. and intro. *A Rainbow for the Christian West*. By Rene Depestre. Amherst: U Massachusetts P, 1977.

Rigby, Graeme. "Publishing Brathwaite: Adventures in Video Style." *World Literature Today* 64.8 (Autumn 1994): 708-714.

Schele, Linda and Mary Ellen Miller. *The Blood of Kings: Dynasty and Ritual in Maya Art.* New York: George Braziller, 1986.

Séjourné, Laurette. *Burning Water: Thought and Religion in Ancient Mexico*. New York: Grove, 1960.

Tedlock, Dennis, trans. and intro. *Popul Vuh: The Mayan Book of the Dawn of Life*. New York: Simon and Schuster, 1985.

Tompkins, Peter. *Mysteries of the Mexican Pyramids*. New York: Harper and Row, 1976.

Torres-Saillant, Silvio. "The Trials of Authenticity in Kamau Brathwaite." *World Literature Today* 64.8 (Autumn 1994): 697-707.

Walmsley, Anne. "Her Stem Singing: Kamau Brathwaite's Zea Mexican Diary: 7 September 1926-7 September 1986." *World Literature Today* 68.4 (Autumn 1994): 747-49.

Weinstein, Norman. "Jazz in the Caribbean Air." *World Literature Today* 68.4 (1994): 714-718.

12

RESTAGING THE PAST:
The Rewriting of
The Tale of the Beautiful Daughter by
Abrahams, Tutuola, Ogali and Aidoo.

by Carmela Garritano

A transcription of the Yoruba tale, "The Girl Who Marries a Monkey," is included in a collection of African folktales in which Roger Abrahams identifies himself as the editor and reteller. In the tale, a beautiful young woman refuses to marry any of the men in the town. One day, she goes off to market and sees the most beautiful man she has ever seen. She decides that she wants him to be her husband. Despite the fact that she has not consulted her parents, she ignores the beautiful man's protests and warnings and follows him out of the marketplace and into the forest. As they proceed further into the forest, he begins to remove parts of his body. First he takes out his teeth; next he peels off his skin, revealing a brown coat of fur, and finally he screeches and jumps at her. She soon realizes she has married a monkey. The monkey forces her up into a tree and rapes her for three days. On the third day a hunter wanders by and sees her. He kills the monkey and returns the beautiful girl to her father. The family begs the hunter to take her as a wife, but he refuses because she has been raped by a monkey, and now may be pregnant.

According to Bernth Lindfors, in 1948, Amos Tutuola, a messenger in the Government Labor Department in Lagos, Nigeria, who was bored with his job, recorded, on pieces of scrap paper, tales he heard as a child from an old man on a palm plantation ("Debts" 224). Four years later *The Palm Wine Drinkard* is published. The book describes the adventures of a palm wine drinkard who travels through towns, forests, and into the underworld in search of his dead palm wine tapster. In an early episode of his journey, the drinkard enters a small town with a large market. He asks the head of the town to assist him in locating his tapster. The man agrees to help, but only if the drinkard will help him rescue his beautiful daughter who was taken from the market by a curious creature. The beautiful daughter, who was due to be married to a man to whom her father gave her, spies a beautiful complete gentleman in the market and decides that this is the man she wants to marry. Despite protests from the complete gentleman, the beautiful girl follows him into the forest. As they move deeper into the forest, the complete gentlemen begins to shed his body parts, which, we learn, were on loan to him. To the horror of the beautiful girl, she soon realizes she has married a skull. The skull locks her in a cave and puts a cowrie around her neck which prevents her from talking. The drinkard finds and rescues her. When he returns her to the village, the father asks him to marry his daughter and he agrees to do so. This, he tells us, is how he obtained is wife.

Ogali Ogali, in 1956, published his play *Veronica My Daughter*. The heroine of the play, Veronica, refuses to accept the old and illiterate, but rich, husband to whom her father has promised her. Instead, she argues that in this day and age, she has the right to select her own husband, and she will marry Mike, a young educated man. Ogali tells his readers in the introduction to his pamphlet that the play "is an attempt to spotlight in form the obstructionist role which some fathers in our society ... play in the love and marriage affairs of their daughters" (138).

Ama Ata Aidoo's play *Anowa* (1965) tells the story of a beautiful woman who, according to her mother, acts just like the young woman in the folktale. Unlike the previous three retellings of the tale of the beautiful daughter, Aidoo does not attempt to tell the tale again. Her postcolonial rewriting creates something entirely new.

In the introduction to *Third World Women and the Politics of Feminism*, Chandra Talpade Mohanty reminds us, "Ideologies of womanhood have as much to do with class and race as they have to do with sex" (13). She insists that Third world feminisms ought to resist positing Third World Woman as a homogeneous category and to disregard "any simple relation of colonizer and colonized, or capitalist and workers" (13). The focus of feminist analysis should be to trace the "multiple intersections or structures of power" which "emphasize the process or form of ruling, not the frozen embodiment of it" (14). Mohanty calls for feminist readings of Third world writing which invoke "the idea of multiple, fluid structures of domination which intersect to locate women differently at particular historical conjunctures" (13). Mohanty is not interested in what Foucault calls "the regulated and legitimate forms of power in their central locations" (Foucault 96). Indeed, she criticizes Western feminist readings of Third world writing which attempt to empower autonomous female selves and in doing so represent the Third World Woman as a "singular, monolithic subject" ("Under Western" 197). Feminist readings of this type erase the "material and historical heterogeneities of the lives of third world women" and reinscribe Third world women within Western humanist discourse. Most importantly, feminist readings which adhere to the Western humanist model fail to account for the ways in which texts mediate and enforce relations of ruling. It is not until we unessentialize and denaturalize individuals and institutions that we can begin to conceptualize oppositional agency. Mohanty argues that only by recognizing "the links among the struggles of Third world women against racism, sexism, colonialism, imperialism and monopoly capital" can we imagine "alliances and collaborations across divisive boundaries" ("Introduction" 4).

Mohanty defines colonization as "a relation of structural domination, and a discursive or political suppression of the heterogeneity of the subject in question" ("Under Western" 196). My reading, and re-writing, of the four re-tellings of "The Tale of the Beautiful Daughter" by Abrahams, Tutuola, Ogali, and Aidoo examines the ways in which the figure of the beautiful woman functions as a stereotype, a discursive figure that struggles to conceal heterogeneity and ambiguity. In an analysis of colonial texts, Homi Bhabha demonstrates how the stereotype "gives access to an 'identity' which is predicated as much on mastery and pleasure as it is on anxiety and defense, for it is a form of multiple and contradictory belief in its recognition of difference and disavowal of it" (75). According to Bhabha, "... the stereotype is a complex, ambivalent, contradictory mode of representation, as anxious as it is assertive, and demands not only that we extend our critical and political objectives but that we change the object of analysis itself" (70). Like Mohanty, Bhabha asks that we shift from reading texts by means of a humanist paradigm which corrects false representations or empowers autonomous selves because it fails to account for the processes through which truths are constructed, normalized, and institutionalized. The focus of our analysis should be toward "an understanding of the approaches of subjectification made possible (and plausible) through stereotypical discourse" (Bhabha 67). He suggests, "The function of ambivalence as one of the most significant discursive and psychical strategies of discriminatory power—whether racist or sexist, peripheral or metropolitan—remains to be charted" (66). By dislodging the contradictions which reside beneath the woman as symbol/stereotype and locating the excess which the stereotype cannot contain, I hope to map "the function of ambivalence" among these four re-tellings of "The Tale of the Beautiful Daughter." The beautiful woman, as she is exchanged among tellers, carries with her the struggles of competing discourses. The movement from one re-telling to the next and the next dislodges the fixity of the symbol and allows us to read the beautiful woman as sign. The repetition of the stereotype, that on which the stereotype depends to insure its truth, becomes, then, that which dismantles its validity. Bhabha names this displacement from symbol to sign "hybridity." It is a third space between sign and symbol which "causes the dominant discourse to split along the axis of its power to be representative" (Bhabha 113). Hybridity allows us to locate those multiple intersections of power Mohanty argues are inextricable from feminist concerns.

The enunciation of culture, much like the production of the stereotype, depends on what Bhabha calls the third space, the hybrid site, or ambivalence. Indeed, the process of cultural differentiation is not one which results in the unearthing and naming of a thing "unitary" in itself (Bhabha 35). Cultural articulation is "a process of signification"(34) which "cannot be sufficient unto itself" (36) because in the "contradictory and ambivalent space of enunciation" the "mirror of representation in which cultural knowledge is customarily revealed" is destroyed (37). The question, becomes "..how, in signifying the present, something comes to be repeated, relocated and translated in the name of tradition, in the guise of a pastness that is not necessarily a faithful sign of historical memory, but a strategy of representing authority" (35). *African Folktales: Traditional Stories of the Black World,* a collection of African folktales compiled and edited by Roger Abrahams, is one instance of cultural signification. Abrahams repeats and relocates the tale as an artifact of African culture. I intend to demonstrate how we might begin to account for the repetition and relocation which Bhabha defines as the enunciation of culture despite Abrahams framing of the tale as a piece of a frozen and authentic Africanness. It is between the stasis which Abrahams assumes and the acts of retelling he veils that we might conceptualize the third space where culture is negotiated.

In the preface to his text, Abrahams labels the compilation "a representative selection of the tales of Black Africa" (xiii). He acknowledges that "representing" a continent as large and diverse as Africa is a difficult task; yet, he contends that his volume manages to illuminate a "cultural unity" which emerges from the "common heritage" of the African experience (xiii) . Clearly, culture, for Abrahams, is what Bhabha calls "an object of empirical knowledge" (Bhabha 34). We can access African culture through a reading of its folktales. Language, according to Abrahams, transcends history, geography and translation, and functions as a transparent medium, capable of capturing some essential Africanness. The author, like the language in which he writes, is a cipher of sorts, distilling the African for his audience.

Abrahams neglects to account for the methods by which the tales he includes in his text were collected. He notes in the preface that a number of the tales have been taken from the writings of missionaries and colonial officials. Others have been transcribed or recorded by anthropologists and folklorists. Abrahams fails to acknowledge not only his own role in the re-writing of each of the tales included in the collection, but the methods by which each tale came to be translated from oral to written text, from Yoruba language to English are not revealed. He erases the lines separating the oral performance of the tale from its transcription, to its place in Abraham's collection where it has been lodged and secured within a category which explains for the reader the function this tale served within its African context. Nonetheless, even as Abrahams argues for a homogeneous and essential African culture, the terms of the very negotiation of the construction of culture reveal themselves. Abrahams concedes that he has "gravitated to the texts that have the greatest impact in the reading, the tales we can enjoy for themselves" (xv), hence calling our attention to his selection of those tales he deems entertaining at the expense of those that cannot be appreciated for themselves. He adds that he has "not hesitated to revise, to attempt to enhance the flow of the narrative" (xv); still, he claims that despite his hand in revising and editing the tales, he has maintained "the distinctive flavor of each, eliminating only those features that made them difficult to read and understand" (xv). We learn that what has been deleted in order to preserve clarity are "the legends, the genealogies, and the histories of the various African cultures" because, according to Abrahams, "histories require too much apparatus to make them understandable"(xvii). For Abrahams, history muddies the cultural, and the kernel of Africanness encapsulated within each tales emerges despite, not through the negotiation with, historical context.

The way Abrahams frames his re-telling of the tale affects our understanding of it, the truth-value we assign to it. The tale of the beautiful daughter, one of the many African folktales compiled in this collection, becomes emblematic of "the courtship-quest sort of tale" (Abrahams 295) or of the tale designed to assist in the "Making a Way Through Life," the section under which Abrahams organizes it in his text. If we, as readers, adhere to the paradigm Abrahams erects for us, we approach the tale as a fixed and enclosed whole. The storyteller, as represented to us, is emblematic of all storytellers in West Africa. Without a historical context, a gender, or name, we cannot differentiate this storyteller from any other, and what remains is one that stands, and speaks, for all.

In the re-telling Abrahams selects, the storyteller acts as teller and reader of the tale. Neither the teller within the story, nor Abrahams, the teller outside the story, allows the performance of the tale to become a site for the negotiation of meaning. The inclusion of the refrain sequences attests to Abrahams's struggle to freeze orality and authenticate his telling. His text transcribes the oral, and he plays the role of ethnographic observer, collecting data unobtrusively. When the audience participates in the performance, they do so by repeating, in unison, the refrains to which the teller has lead them. Unlike tales which resist closure and invite debate, the telling of "The Girl who Married a Monkey" becomes an occasion for instruction and for the normalizing of proper codes of conduct. The narrator informs us that since girls have been selecting their own husbands, "they are the ones who initiate the matter—and trouble along with it" (337). When the girl realizes she has married a monkey, the storyteller interrupts the telling to remind us that "a child born in good house is spoiled so much that she knows nothing about the world. Friends, let no one spoil his child through overindulgence" (342). We are encouraged to celebrate the rape of the daughter by participating in the mockery. We are told she is forced to copulate like an animal, made to eat food to which she is not accustomed and slapped for complaining, and after "the terrible predicament" of the rape is described, the narrator gleans the message for us: "So ever since that day, when we give our child advice, she should listen closely to what we have to say" (343).

Gayatri Spivak notes, "Between patriarchy and imperialism, subject-constitution and object-formation, the figure of the woman disappears, not into a pristine nothingness, but into a violent shuttling which is the displaced figuration of the 'third-world woman' caught between tradition and modernization" (102). Abraham's re-writing of "The Girl who Marries a Monkey" posits itself as an authentic expression of the African identity. Within the tale, that African identity is secured through the figure of the woman. The reinscription of her desire into a "traditional" patriarchal economy re-affirms Africanness through violence enacted upon the female body. As Spivak shows, the woman is lost in the shuttle between those discourses through which she is written.

Embedded within Amos Tutuola's *The Palm Wine Drinkard*, we find another re-telling of the tale of the beautiful daughter. Tutuola's re-writing differs from Abrahams's in several significant ways. Tutuola does not present himself as an ethnographer who has collected and recorded oral artifacts from Africa. He translates an oral into a written text and constructs something on the border between an oral performance and a novel; several critics have placed his text in this third space. Chantal Zabus, for example, labels *The Palm Wine Drinkard* a "folk-novel" which "precariously straddles the world of orature and that of literature and bridges the two by translating the one into the other" (108). Bernth

Lindfors calls the text "a cleverly woven string of loosely connected episodes, many of which appear to have been borrowed or derived from folktales and embellished with details from the technology of modern civilization" (*Folklore* 59). Viktor Beilis refuses to grant the text the status of novel, but reads it as "a narration of myth and fairy tales of the Yoruba people to which the author belongs" (448). Instead of articulating his retelling as a replica of an original oral source, Tutuola constructs an exchange between discourses.

The Palm Wine Drinkard bares the marks of what Zabus describes as a "triple translation" from oral to written text, Yoruba to English and from its address to a local audience to composition for an international readership (109). His text exists in the interstices of West African and European discourses and, like a palimpsest, holds layers of meanings which despite erasure, leave imprints. Zabus argues of West African texts written in English: " ...behind the scriptural authority of the European language, the earlier, imperfectly erased remnants of the African language can still be perceived" (Zabus 3). Each of these critics analyzes Tutuola's use of language, sifting through his imperfect English to uncover fragments of an Yoruba tradition. I want to focus on Tutuola's insertion of the tale of the beautiful daughter, but not in order to extricate the African from the Western. I intend to argue that between the layers of discourse, the beautiful daughter still, in Spivak's words, does not speak.

Unlike the storyteller in "The Girl Who Married a Monkey," the narrator in *The Palm Wine Drinkard* encourages the audience to sympathize with the plight of the beautiful daughter. Her actions are not excused, but we are asked to understand and forgive her. The drinkard himself absolves her from responsibility. He explains, "I would not blame the lady for following the skull as a complete gentleman to his house at all. Because if I were a lady, no doubt I would follow him to wherever he would go" (207). He, too, is seduced by the beauty of the complete gentleman. He tells his readers, "After I looked at him for so many hours, then I ran to a corner of the market and I cried for a few minutes because I thought within myself why was I not created with beauty as this gentleman, but when I remembered that he was only a skull, then I thanked God that he had created me without beauty" (207). The lady's beauty, like that of "an angel" (201), prevents her from wanting to marry any of the men to whom her father tries to give her. Her extraordinary, god-given beauty, and the complete gentleman's enchanting, though borrowed, exterior, excuse her impropriety.

Tutuola's version of the tale palliates the daughter's deviance and the reactions of the other characters in the tale to it. The reprimand comes not from the narrator or her father, but from the mouth of the daughter herself.

The narrator explains that "When the lady saw that she remained with only skull, she began to say that her father had been telling her to marry a man, but she did not listen to or believe him" (204). She realizes her mistake and tries to escape "to return to her father's town, but she was not allowed by this fearful creature at all" (204). Furthermore, the girl is not raped by the skull as a punishment for her desires. Tutuola makes it clear that no sexual violence was enacted upon the daughter. The skull, we are told, has a wife and children to which he attends while the daughter remains alone and tied in the cave. In the end, she is not an unmarriageable outcast who has caused her family great shame, and the audience/readership is not invited to laud her suffering. She is welcomed back into her father's house and the community and, finally, married by her hero, the narrator.

The influence of Tutuola's Christian beliefs on his writing has been commented upon by many critics. Lindfors reminds us that, in fact, Tutuola first submitted his manuscript to Lutterworth press, a missionary publisher for the United Society for Christian Literature ("Amos" 637). Although Lutterworth did not accept the manuscript, two of its publishers passed it on to Faber and Faber, the publishing company that did rewrite and then publish the novel. Clearly, Tutuola Christianizes his retelling of the tale. He constructs an ameliorated version and encourages his audience to forgive the crimes of the daughter. Her actions are not condoned, however. We are reminded that before she was lured from the market by the beauty of the skull, "this lady totally refused to marry that man who was introduced to her by her father" (201). Beauty seduces and female desire disrupts. As Brian Massumi, in his writing/reading of Deleuze and Guattari, points out, "Gender is a fatal detour from desire-in-deviation .... Gender is a form of imprisonment, a socially functional limitation of a body's connective and transformative capacity" (87). Although the beautiful daughter escapes rape and is accepted as a wife, she, finally, is absorbed into the male economy. The transformative capacity of female desire is forgiven, but domesticated.

Ogali Ogali's play *Veronica My Daughter* moves from a rural West African space to the urban environment. The text itself is categorized as an Onitsha market pamphlet, or African popular literature. I use the term "popular" carefully. As Lindfors notes, "In Africa popular literature is not mass literature because the masses cannot all read the same language or else cannot read at all" (*Popular* 1). Market literature reaches a literate and "an urbanized, acculturated elite, and their reading tastes tend to reflect their new interests and enthusiasms as well as their adjustments to conflicting sets of values and to modern life" (1). The market pamphlet industry emerged in the Onitsha market in Nigeria after the Second World

War, and after a brief period of decline after the Biafran war and the shelling of the market in 1967, flourishes today (25).

The pamphlets, as has been argued by many critics, respond to the tumultuous social climate of post World War Two Nigeria. Virginia Coulon argues, "The greatest concern of these authors is helping their readers ease over the obstacles of their everyday life in an urban environment" (310). Pamphlet literature does more than describe "the problems of a changing society"; it "attempts to provide some kind of guidance and direction to the masses of the people caught in the violence and confusion arising from the changes" (Obiechina 16). Gerald Porter contends that the pamphlets promote a "specific model, the self-sufficient individual" (173). What Porter disregards is how his "individual" is gendered in the pamphlets. The individual is male, and, Stephanie Newell argues, seeped in masculinism, "that strand of masculinity where the artist anxiously re-invents and re-presents women to a male addressee, adapting old gender models to maintain male control of changing social and cultural formations" (50). Newell demarcates the ways pamphlet literature stereotypes women. She contends that "by stereotyping femininity, narrators attempt to fix it, warn against it, and disarm it in a rapidly urbanizing context" (53).

Veronica My Daughter adheres to the ideology Newell calls masculinism. Although Ogali Ogali's play does not declare, explicitly, that females are morally degenerate, and subsequently warn its male readers against lascivious women, Ogali's rewriting of the tale of the beautiful daughter reiterates the male/female binary on which such proclamations depend. Under the veil of creating a work which alleges to embrace modern, liberal values and argue for a woman's right to choose her husband, Ogali silences the daughter in much the same fashion as do Abrahams and Tutuola. Her desire is re-configured into the patriarchal framework, absorbed by sameness.

The play opens with a familiar dilemma. Veronica is of marriageable age but refuses to marry the man to whom her father has bequeathed her. Veronica tells her friends, "Well friends, my opinion is that I must get married as soon as the year comes to an end. This does not mean I am to marry any person who presents himself as a prospective husband. I am in love with a young boy and am sure you know what it means to fall in love with someone of your choice" (141). In modern Nigeria, a woman can select her own husband for love. No longer does she have to marry one of the village boys, nor does she have to accept the hand of the man whom her father wishes her to marry. She has the right to choose.

The tale valorizes education, revealed by one's ability to speak and write standard English. Veronica tells us that her "old illiterate father," who did not even attend "infant school," wants her to be wed to "one old-money monger of the first order whose name is Chief Bassey, a grade one illiterate" (142). The "uncooked English" (142) of Chiefs Jombo and Bassey illustrates their backwardness. The play collapses, and demeans, their adherence to traditional values, their Pidgin English and their fight to restrict Veronica's freedom.   Conversely, Mike, Veronica's lover, is admired because he is educated and he encourages Veronica to continue with her education, despite what her father and brothers say. Pauline, Veronica's mother, sides with her daughter, and admonishes her husband for limiting her opportunities: "While you discouraged me from reading any further, Mike is encouraging Vero to read further" (144). She warns her husband not to "take for granted that Vero must repeat the mistake I made"(160). She describes her own marriage to an uneducated man as a "suicide," and assures her husband that "Vero must avoid it as far as I am alive" (160).

The written word, representative of a civilized society, wields power in Ogali's play. Newell notes of market literature in general, "The written word is treated by authors as that which reflects final truths, arresting the confusing blur of city faces to identify causes and character types" (56). In *Veronica My Daughter*, letters transport truth. It is through letters that Veronica and Mike tell the other of their love and their determination to marry, and Veronica's brothers write to Mike to warn him of their disapproval of his intentions toward their sister. The Law, the ultimate expression of the authority of the written word, decides how the conflict will be resolved. The power of Law and Education merge in the character of Mark Johnson, Headmaster of the Public School and Chairman of the District Council. He instructs Chief Jombo in the Law, assuring him that "it is illegal if you force her to marry contrary to her wish" (162). He continues: "My friend, it appears you do not know what is going on in this country. Let me tell you that one part of this matter has been solved and that is the question of Mike marrying Vero. According to recent Law passed by the Government, Mike is entitled to pay thirty pounds—nothing more, nothing less" (163). The word of the Law and the Literate is final. Chief Jombo concedes and thanks Johnson "for wetin you don teacham me today. Dat mean I say for don go prison if me I no learn wetin you teacham em today" (165).

The Law, through its male voice, instructs Veronica's father to permit her to choose her husband. The traditional practice of paying a bride price of more than thirty dollars has been made illegal by colonial authorities, and so the rights of women are protected from the subservient role to which they were relegated by the traditional African way of life. In fact, Veronica's ability to act according to her own "will" signifies how "civilized" and "modern" Africa has become. Spivak writes, "… the protection of woman (today the 'third-world woman') becomes a signifier for the establishment of a good society which must, at such inaugurative moments, transgress mere legality, or equity of legal policy" (94). Even though Ogali's character Veronica has the right to choose her husband, she functions only as a signifier through which the discourses of First World/Third World wrangle. The patriarchal modernist framework remains the same. Only the definitions change, and what occurs is "the redefinition as a crime of what had been tolerated, known, or adulated as ritual" (Spivak 94). The ritual of paying a brideprice is now a crime, and although the play presents this as an advance for women, it does so through the voices of men, namely Veroncia's husband and Mark Johnson. As Newell notes, "If Veronica chooses her husband, Michael, against her father's will, both masculinities encircle her" (61). Ogali Ogali advocates a dismissal of the backward ways of a rural and traditional Africa in favor of Western values which, under the guise of free will, facilitates only the exchange of the beautiful daughter from illiterate father to educated husband.

Although Ogali defends the rights of women, Veronica *functions* within the text as a symbol in much the same way as the figure of the beautiful daughter *functions*, symbolically, in the texts of Abrahams and Tutuola. Abraham's translation of the tale re-inscribes the daughter within African tradition. The tale represents the voice of traditional West African culture and institutionalizes the gendered restraints that patriarchal culture enforces; it warns women to obey their fathers because if they shun traditional instruction, they will be punished. Tutuola's Christianized re-telling of the tale does not castigate the daughter for disobeying tradition. Her impropriety is explained and forgiven. Nonetheless, at the tale's conclusion, the daughter re-renters the patriarchal economy when her father rewards the narrator for rescuing his daughter by giving his daughter to him as a wife. Despite her conduct, and to the credit of his character, the narrator accepts the offer and marries the beautiful daughter. The patriarchal economy remains intact and is re-articulated through the daughter. Female desire, represented as deviancy in the stereotype of the beautiful daughter, is finally controlled.

In each of the retellings of "The Tale of the Beautiful Daughter," the female figure acts as a stereotype. She is a figure to be mastered; yet, as Bhabha explains, the taking up of any one position is as much a site of fantasy as of fixity (77). The ambivalence on which the stereotype depends, ambivalence that grows out of the re-telling of the tale, is that which it struggles to conceal in order to shore up its claim to truth. The lessons encapsulated in and the behaviors normalized by the figure of beautiful daughter have truth-value only if her figure is representative, only if it denies what Bhabha calls "the play of difference" (75). Ambivalence and difference, however, disrupts the stereotype's "truth." My reading of the three re-tellings of the tale attempts to facilitate this disruption by examining how each version of the tale represents the actions and responses of the beautiful daughter differently. Yet, in each text she functions symbolically, as a stereotype, in the same way. The daughter of Abraham's re-telling refuses to obey tradition and is punished. Tutuola's daughter admits her mistake and is forgiven. Ogali's character argues for a woman's right to act independently, and the play defends her decision to ignore tradition and embrace the "enlightened" ways of the West. Yet, the daughter only mimics the cultural codes offered by patriarchy. Through the character of the beautiful daughter, we have traced the intersection of discourses which construct her, but do not allow her to speak or act.

Carole Boyce Davies reads Ama Ata Aidoo's play *Anowa* as "a kind of theorizing within the creative text" (60). The play acts as a "contemporary theoretical exploration of colonial discourses and female subjectivity" (60). Bhabha, I think, allows us to explore in what ways Aidoo does indeed theorize through Anowa. For Bhabha, "... the event of theory becomes the negotiation of contradictory and antagonistic instances that open up hybrid sites and objectives of struggle, and destroy those negative polarities between knowledge and its objects, and between theory and practical-political reason" (25). I offer this brief, and by no means conclusive, discussion of Aidoo's rewriting of the tale of the beautiful daughter as an instance of rewriting which is not simply what Lyotard calls a remembering, a "seeking out, designating and naming the hidden facts" (28), but a rewriting which "presupposes that the past itself is the actor or agent that gives to the mind the elements with which the scene will be constructed" (30). Aidoo does not return to the tale as an original source, nor does she rework the tale for an international or African urban readership. She refers back to the telling of the tale and, by doing so, conceptualizes culture not as an unveiling, but as a negotiation carried out in the act of cultural enunciation itself.

One way to illuminate the difference between Aidoo's *performance* of the tale and, for example, Ogali's play about the beautiful daughter, is to examine how each author frames her/his telling. Ogali, like Abrahams, presents his text as an authentic expression of African culture. He freezes cultural expression. He assures his audience that the "originality—with African background—and simple style" of his play make it "the most popular drama ever written by an African" (138). Ogali represents the meaning of his play as an object, static and homogenous. He writes, "Veronica deserves praise for denouncing wealthy Chief Bassey, in preference to poor Mike, the apple of her eye" (138). Aidoo, on the other hand, foregrounds the heterogeneous character of the performance of *Anowa*. Although she provides production notes, she concedes, "It is not necessary to follow closely the instructions set down" (63). Indeed, the ending of the play is negotiable. Aidoo explains that the director can elect "to end the play with the final exit of Anowa" or "follow the script"; "The choice is open" (63). Aidoo highlights the performance of her play. Performance, according to Helen Gilbert, "defers and deflects the authority of any written version" and as a form is "ephemeral, latent, potential"(107). Unlike Abrahams, who authorizes his text by connecting its validity to a permanent and authentic African culture, Aidoo, again in Gilbert's words on performance, "sets up the dialogic process that post-colonial representations of history must engage in if they are to operate counter-discursively" (107).

In the opening scene of the play, Aidoo foregrounds her rewriting. The Old Woman in the Prologue tells her husband, "That Anowa is something else! Like all the beautiful maidens in the tales, she has refused to marry any of the sturdy men who have asked for her hand in marriage. No one knows what is wrong with her!" (67). Anowa's mother, after learning that her daughter wants to marry Kofi, criticizes her by accusing her of behaving "like the girl in the folk tale" (75).

Anowa is an outsider within the community, and, eventually, within her marriage. Osam, her father, reminds Anowa's mother, who is angered by her daughter's choice of a husband, "I have always asked you to apprentice her to a priestess to quiet her down" (71). He says, "My wife, people with better vision than yours or mine have seen that Anowa is not like you or me" (73). Kofi, her husband, attempts to discourage Anowa from traveling on the road with him: "This life is not good for a woman. No not even a woman like you" (83). He continues, "You ought to have been born a man" (84). Her inability to have children stems from the fact that her "soul is too restless"(88).

Anowa's transgressive desire to select her own husband, to work with him, and finally to refuse to have slaves resists inscription by patriarchy, traditional values, or the capitalist marketplace. Anowa remains on the outside and, from that position, acts and speaks. Like the witch or priestess, she is "a source of transgressive power" (Davies 74). It is her critique from the margins that allows us to envision the intersections of power which Mohanty argues operate in the writings of third world women. Kofi's desire to own slaves collides with his masculinism. When Anowa protests, he dismisses her by reminding her that she is "a woman and I am a man" (90). Anowa's refusal to participate in the exploitation of other human beings, as Davies suggests, "challenges his capitalist project and its implications that it activates patriarchal rules" (64). Her fondness for "looking for the common pain and general wrong," Kofi warns her, prevents her from bringing her "mind home" (99). He asks her to accept his taking of slaves, to "be happy in being my wife and maybe we shall have our own children" (99).

Anowa refuses to submit, to conform to the role of silent and dutiful wife. She instead remembers, and rewrites, a recurrent dream, and in her reassembling of the pieces, is disruptive. She was told, as a child, "not to mention the dream again" (107). We learn that after recounting the dream to her parents "there was talk of apprenticing me to a priestess" (107). Before the dream began, Anowa barraged her grandmother with a series of questions about "The pale men" who "built the big houses to keep the slaves" (105). Her grandmother orders her to forget because "All good men and women try to forget" (106). That which is forgotten, or repressed, refuses to be erased. Anowa dreams that she is a "big woman" riddled with holes "out of which poured men, women, and children" (106). As the men and women pour out of her body, she dreams that, other men and women come and seize them and stamp upon them (106). Anowa's red swollen body bursts, and when she awoke, she was told "not to mention the dream again" (107).

The rewriting of the dream in the play signifies Anowa's refusal to be absorbed into the partiarchal economy and to be silent. The dream, outside of Symbolic existence and language, dismantles the history which erases slavery. Female desire, represented by Anowa's red and swollen pubescent body in the dream, the body out of which human beings emerge, is the transgressive force which refuses to forget, but which is silenced by the community. The dream, Anowa remembers, in fact, initiates "talk of apprenticing me to a priestess" (107). And as Davies suggests, the dream also recalls "the metaphoric convergence of the dark continent as Africa and the African woman" (78). Aidoo re-writes the metaphor "between Mother and Africa in nationalist discourses" (Davies 79) and uses the image to represent something horrible, unspeakable, abject. Anowa's dream conflates becoming a woman and experiencing desire with the taking of human beings as slaves. "The link between woman and slavery— 'traffic in women' and 'traffic in slaves'—contained in the dream and carried throughout the text" (Davies 78). However, the telling of the dream and the disregarding of the order to be silent, the process out of which the dream is told, is as powerful an act of resistance as the remembering itself.

Aidoo, according to Vincent Odamitten, reminds us of "the complicity and active participation of Africa people in that degrading trafficking of human flesh" (52). Aidoo also refuses to contain slavery within a simple First World/Third World binary. Kofi's active part in the keeping of slaves is linked to the trading of slaves by "pale men," but not deemed either less or more morally reprehensible. What is more significant is the intersections between Kofi's attempts to silence his wife and his defense of slavery. Sexism and capitalism collide in the play, and we are positioned in a space from which we can view what Mohanty called "the links among struggles" ("Introduction" 4).

Anowa's position as an outsider, as a wayfarer, a woman who is not quite a woman and not quite a man, enables her to disturb normality and the oppressive strictures through which it is secured. Unlike the beautiful daughter in the folktale, Anowa refuses to be placed in her father's house or married and silenced. Aidoo's play does not conclude when the girl marries. The nontraditional marriage of Anowa and Kofi, "the new husband and ... the new wife" (87), cannot contain female desire. That desire which is deemed threatening to the social order in the three previous retellings, here, is a transgressive force. *Anowa* is what Homi Bhabha labels a "borderline work of culture." It "demands an encounter with 'newness' that is not part of the continuum of past and present. It creates a sense of the new as an insurgent act of cultural translation. Such art does not merely recall the past as social cause or aesthetic precedent; it renews the past, refiguring it as a contingent 'in-between' space, that innovates and interrupts the performance of the present" (Bhabha 7). Unlike the three re-tellings of the tale by Abrahams, Tutuola, and Ogali, Aidoo's rewriting resists fixity and closure. It articulates self-consciously the space in which cultural, racial, sexual, and gendered identities are negotiated. In this space, Aidoo allows the beautiful woman a voice; female desire, which is read and naturalized as dangerous and deviant in the other re-tellings, is that force which interrupts the performance of the present.

WORKS CITED

Abrahams, Roger. *African Folktales*. New York: Pantheon Books, 1983.

Aidoo, Ama Ata. *Two Plays: The Dilemma of a Ghost and Anowa*. New York: Longman, 1987.

Beilis, Viktor. "Ghosts, People, and Books of Yorubaland." *Research in African Literatures* 18.4 (1987): 447-57.

Bhabha, Homi K. *The Location of Culture*. London and New York: Routledge, 1994.

Coulon, Virginia. "Onitsha Goes National: Nigerian Writing in Macmillan's Pacesetter Series." *Research in African Literatures* 18.3 (1987): 304-19.

Davies, Carole Boyce. *Black Women, Writing, and Identity: Migrations of the Subject.* London and New York: Routledge, 1994.

Foucault, Michel. *Power/Knowledge: Selected Interviews and Other Writings 1972-1977.* Ed. Colin Gordon. Trans. Colin Gordon, Leo Marshall, John Mepham and Kate Soper. New Yprk: Pantheon Books, 1980.

Gilbert, Helen. "De-Scribing Orality: Performance and the Recuperation of Voice." *De-Scribing Empire: Post-colonialism and Identity.* Eds. Chris Tiffin and Alan Lawson. Routledge: London and New York, 1994.

Lindfors, Bernth. "Amos Tutuola: Debts and Assets." *Critical Perspectives on Amos Tutuola.* London: Heinemann, 1975.

_______ "Amos Tutuola: Literary Syncretism and the Yoruba Folk Tradition." *European-Language Writing in Sub-Saharan Africa.* Ed. Albert S. Gerard. Budapest: Akademiaia Kiado, 1986.

_______ *Popular Literatures in Africa.* Trenton: Africa World Press, 1991.

Lyotard, Jean-Francois. *The Inhuman: Reflections on Time.* Trans. Geoffrey Bennington and Rachel Bowlby. Stanford: Stanford UP, 1991.

Massumi, Brian. *A User's Guide to Capitalism and Schizophrenia: Deviations from Deleuze and Guattari.* Cambridge: MIT Press, 1993.

Mohanty, Chandra Talpade. "Introduction: Cartogrphies of Struggle - Third Wold Women and the Politics of Feminism." *Third World Women and the Politics of Feminism.* Eds. Chandra Talpade Mohanty, Ann Russo and Lourdes Torres. Bloomington: Indiana UP, 1991.

_______ "Under Western Eyes: Feminist Scholarship and Colonial Discourses." *Colonial Discourse and Post-Colonial Theory: A Reader.* Eds. Patrick Williams and Laura Chrisman. New York: Columbia University Press, 1994.

Newell, Stephanie. "From the Brink of Oblivion: The Anxious Masculinism of Nigerian Market Literatures." *Research in African Literatures* 27.3 (1996): 50-67.

Obiechina, Emmanuel. *An African Popular Literature: A Study of Onitsh Market Pamphlets.* Cambridge UP, 1973.

Odamitten, Vincent O. *The Art of Ama Ata Aidoo: Polylectics and Reading Against Neocolonialism.* Gainesville: University Press of Florida, 1994.

Ogali, Ogali. *Veronica My Daughter and Other Onitsha Plays and Stories.* Eds. Reinhrd W. Sander and Peter K. Ayers. Washington, D.C., Three Continents Press, 1980.

Porter, Gerald. "Market Forces: Onitsha Pamphlets and the Postcolonial Experience." *Signs and Signals: Popular Culture in Africa.* Ed. Raoul Granqvist. Stockholm: Umea, 1990.

Spivak, Gayatri Chakravorty. "Can the Subaltern Speak?" *Colonial Discourse and Post-Colonial Theory: A Reader.* Eds. Patrick Williams and Laura Chrisman. New York: Columbia UP, 1994.

Tutuola, Amos. *The Palm-Wine Drinkard and My Life in the Bush of Ghosts.* New York: Grove Press, 1994.

13

RACE, GENDER, AND ISLAM
In Two North African Folktales:
Marguerite Taos Amrouche's
"Le Grain Magique" and
Abdelaziz Aroui's
"The Black Merchant"

by Lamia Ben Youssef

My paper analyzes race and gender in two North African folktales: "The Black Merchant" by Abdelaziz Aroui, and "The Magical Grain," by Marguerite Taos Amrouche. Using Vladimir Propp's theory of the folktale, and Julia Kristeva's notion of the abject, I shall demonstrate that the North African slave narrative, though narrated from the oppressor's perspective, is paradoxically the site of resistance and conformity to the dominant Islamic ideology. My analysis turns on two axes: the way these folktales display conformity and resistance and the relation of blackness to the feminine and the abject.

"The Black Merchant" is the story of an Arab caravan owner who gets fleeced by a cunning black merchant. Like Iachimo in Shakespeare's *Cymbeline*, the deceitful black merchant pushes the Arab man to make a bet over his wife's chastity. If the Black merchant is able to give him proof of her infidelity, the Arab merchant will lose all his property to the black man. With the complicity of Settoute, a wicked old woman, the black merchant manages to get a caftan from the merchant's wife, which he presents as the proof of her infidelity, thus causing the ruin of the Arab merchant. Worried about her husband's absence, the faithful wife sends her maid after him. As soon as the story of his misfortune reaches her, the faithful wife decides to get back her husband's fortune. She asks her faithful slave to buy 100 camels, 99 slaves, goods, men's clothes and a stamp bearing her name. Disguised as a man, the wife heads for the town where the black merchant lives. At the sight of the new prey, the black merchant invites the disguised wife to his house. During dinner, the wife drugs the black merchant, marks his body with her stamp, and leaves for the Sultan's palace, where she accuses him of being a run-away slave. The black merchant is summoned to court. Upon the discovery of the wife's stamp on his body, the Cadi (judge) orders the restoration of the slave and the fortune he has accumulated to his master. Later, the faithful wife reveals to the husband her true identity. She gives the black merchant his freedom, but dispossesses him of the fortune he has earned by guile and deceit.

"The Magical Grain" deals with the story of seven brothers who exile themselves, leaving behind an old mother and a newly born sister after Settoute, a wicked old woman, has deceptively told them their mother has delivered a son. At the age of fifteen, the daughter decides to look for her brothers. The mother gives her daughter food, a horse, a slave woman, a magical grain, and warns her against bathing in and drinking from the fountain of the blacks (i.e., the one used exclusively by the blacks). On the first days of the journey, the mother's voice would come through the magical grain to reassure her daughter. The more she and her slave advance in the desert, the harder it is to hear the mother's voice. When they arrive at the two fountains—the fountain of the whites and the fountain of the blacks—the white girl loses the magical grain. Forgetting her mother's warning, she bathes in the fountain of the blacks and lets her slave bathe in the fountain of whites. To her horror, the mistress becomes black and the slave white. When they reach the village where the seven brothers live, the black servant usurps the sister's identity. After a while, the brothers discover that the camels are thin and sick. Suspecting a spell, the little brother decides to spy on his sister's slave. After listening to her plaintive songs, he discovers her plight, and tells his other brothers about it. Unable to tell who their real sister is, the seven brothers consult a wise man who advises them to compare the hair of the two women. The slave woman is unmasked and put to death at the request of the white girl. The latter regains her whiteness by bathing in the water of the white women's fountain. The following spring, mallow plants have grown where the slave woman's ashes are buried. The sister cooks the plants for her brothers. The seven brothers are instantly transformed into ravens and the girl into a dove.

In Theory and History of Folklore, Vladimir Propp argues that folklore is an ideological discipline that arises from the clash of two ages or systems and their ideologies:

Inherited folklore comes into conflict with the old system that created it and denies this system. It does not deny the old system directly but rather the images created by it, transforming them into their opposites or giving them a reverse, disparaging, negative coloring. The once sacred is transformed into the hostile, the great into the harmful, evil, or monstrous. But sometimes the old is preserved without any noticeable changes and gets along peacefully with new forms and relations. Folklore enters into contradiction with itself, and such contradictions are always present.(11)

Underlying "The Black Merchant" and "The Magical Grain" is a clash between the values of an old matrilineal order and those of the Islamic patriarchal system. The coexistence of these two systems explains why the two tales both conform to and resist Islamic patriarchy.

In *Women and Gender in Islam/Historical Roots of a Modern Debate*, Leila Ahmed asserts the existence of a matriarchal society in pre-Islamic Arabia. She notes the existence of an uxorilocal practice in Muhammad's own background. "Muhammad's mother, Amina, remained with her clan after her marriage with 'Abdullah, who visited her there, and after Muhammad's birth... passed to the care of his parental kin only after her death (43). Also the economic independence of Khedija (Muhammad's first wife); "her marriage overture; to a man many years younger than herself; and her monogamous marriage as solely legitimate reflect Jahilia rather than Islamic practice" (42). In *Beyond the Veil*, Fatima Mernissi also explains how Islam banished the old matrilineal unions by condemning them as *Zina* (adultery):

> Ibn Saad (Kitab al-Tabakat) held that the Muslim family marked a break with earlier practices. They acknowledged that the patriarchal marriage endorsed by Islam had been paralleled by many other forms of union that were clearly anti-patriarchal: there were unions in which the child does not belong to the biological father (and even polyandrous marriages in which the woman had more than one regular sexual partner), and there were unions in which the woman had an absolute right to send her husband away if she so desired, severing the marital bond with a ritual gesture as simple as lowering a veil across the mouth of her when she no longer wished her husband to enter. (*Beyond the Veil* 66)

Both Mernissi and Ahmed point to women's resistance to Islam during Muhamad's life and after his death. And they cite as an example the incident of the harlots of Hadramaut, a movement of apostasy led by a group of women who celebrated the Prophet's death with the drum. According to Mernissi, these women were not harlots as Islamic history presents them, but aristocratic women who opposed Islam because it jeopardized their position:

The Muslim text dismisses them summarily as harlots. But this "harlotry" was unusual indeed. The Muslim historian Ibn Habib al-Baghdadi identifies twelve of them. Two were grandmothers, one a mother, and seven were young girls. Three of the twelve belonged to the ashraf (the noble class) and four to the tribe of kinda, a royal tribe which provided Yemen with its Kings... The opposition between these women and Islam was clearly grounded on the sexual field. The fact that the caliph (Abu Bakr) labeled his opponents as harlots implies that Islam condemned their sexual practice whatever they were, as harlotry. I believe that the incident of the harlots of Hadramaut is an example of Islam's opposition to prevailing sexual practices in pre-Islamic Arabia. (*Beyond the Veil* 72-73)

Through their demonization of the feminine, the two tales conform to the discourse of Islamic orthodoxy. Indeed, the entire Muslim social structure can be seen as an attack on, and a defense against the disruptive power of female sexuality. In *The Revivication of Religious Sciences*, the eleventh-century theologist and philosopher Imam al-Ghazali sees civilization as a struggle to contain women's destructive power. Societies prosper only if we create institutions "that foster male dominance through sexual segregation and polygamy" (Mernissi, *Beyond the Veil* 32). Unlike Freud's "machismo theory" where women derive pleasure from suffering and submission to the man's conquest, "the implicit theory of female sexuality, as seen in Imam al-Ghazali's interpretation of the Koran, casts the woman as the hunter and the man as the passive victim" (*Beyond the Veil* 33). He perceives her *kaid*, "[her] power to deceive and defeat men by cunning and intrigue," as destructive of the Muslim social order:

It is therefore no surprise that in the actively sexual Muslim female aggressiveness is seen as turned outward. The nature of her aggression is precisely sexual. The Muslim woman is endowed with a fatal attraction which erodes the male's will to resist her and reduces him to a passive acquiescent role. He has no choice; he can only give in to her attraction, whence her identification with fitna, chaos, and with the anti-divine and anti-social forces of the universe. (41)

In both tales, Settoute is presented as a threat to the established Islamic order. In "The Black Merchant's Tale," the old woman Settoute is responsible for the white merchant's misfortune. Without her complicity and cunning, the black Merchant would have lost the bet. Disguised as a beggar, she asks the faithful wife to give her clothes for her daughter's hopechest. The wife ignores her at first, then on the eighth day, she gives her the caftan, which she gives to the black merchant in exchange of five hundred golden coins. In "The Magical Grain," Settoute disrupts the patriarchal order by precipitating the departure of the seven brothers. To get rid of them, she tells them their mother delivered a boy who can take care of her.

As in the teachings of al-Ghazali, women's morality in Aroui's text seems contingent upon their confinement. Enumerating the virtues of his wife, the husband boasts that no one has ever seen her face; for she never leaves her house, not even to visit her family. A similar point is made when the black merchant reaches the white merchant's house. Noticing the grass growing on the door step, he concludes that this wife is not going to be easily seduced.

In Islamic tradition, there are two kinds of *zina* (adultery): *zina al 'ain* (*zina* of the eye), and *zina al-udhuni* (*zina* of the ear). "It is forbidden to the Muslim [to see or] take pleasure in the harmonious voice of a woman who is not his" (Abdelwahab Bouhdiba, *Sexuality in Islam* 39). The whole story of the bet falls within Islamic patriarchy's view that "the married woman whose husband is absent is a particular threat to men." As one hadith says: "Do not go to the women whose husbands are absent. Because Satan will get in your bodies as blood rushes through your blood" *(Beyond the Veil* 42). In addition to confinement, the internalization of patriarchy's ethics serves to curb the dangerous sexuality of married women. Describing the virtues of the merchant's wife, the narrator states that she is one of those "strong, stallion-like women, who can take revenge and defeat men" (Aroui 113).

It is worth noting that Settoute is a recurrent figure in North African folklore. In the two folktales, the demonization of the wicked old woman "Settoute" points to Patriarchy's demonization of the matriarchal societies existing in North Africa before the establishment of Islam. The Islamicization of the Roman province of Ifriqiya (namely, comtemporary Tunisia and Algeria) involved bloody wars between Muslim Arabs and the Berber Queen Kahina. In *The Berbers in Arabic Literature*, H.T. Norris notes that in Arabic history and literature, Kahina (prophetess) appears as a "Maghrebi Boudicca, a combination of Cleopatra and Bilqis the Queen of Sheba, who defeated the Muslim troops at Wadi Tarda in 688-9"(49). It is reported that she plotted the assassination of Uqba Ibn Nafi', the Muslim leader who conquered Ifriqiya (51). In 701, she was defeated by Hassen al-Nu'maan, who "cut off her head near a well which henceforth bore the name of the Kahina's well" (52). The murder of Kahina gave birth to many legends. In Maghrebi folklore, the female villain always appears near a fountain or a well. In "The Magical Grain," and "Aisha the Daughter of the Fisherman," Settoute appears near a fountain. In "The Stories of the Seven Dannu Sisters,"[1] Settoute kills her grandsons Hassan and Hussein (names of the sons of Caliph Ali, Muhammad's son-in-law) and incites her daughter to rebellion against her husband. In "The Black Merchant's

Tale," the name Settoute is always followed by a curse: "May she never rest in peace."

The repression of the feminine ought to be viewed within the context of monotheistic Islam which condemns the worshiping of the female deities, Manat, Allat, and Uzza, and dismisses the matriarchal societies in Jahiliya as a period of paganism and ignorance. The connivance between blacks and women in the two tales is due to the polytheism of the black slaves who were brought from Bilad al-Sudan, Kanem-Borno, Lake Chad, and Kano (contemporary northern Nigeria) (J.O. Hunwick, 25-26). The conflated fear of blackness and the feminine is best illustrated in the letter Ahmad Baba al-Tumbuktawi addressed to Hammuda Pasha (1782-1814) in 1800. In "The Uncovering of the Hidden Atheism of the Blacks of Tunisia," Ahmad Baba—a Black Muslim theologist—warns the Husseinid ruler that the "behavior of those Negroes will mark the ruin of this land (Rached Limam 354). Explaining the context of this letter, Limam writes:

> The number of Blacks in Tunisia increased in the second half of the eighteenth century. Although some of them had become converted to Islam, they did not lose their old pagan beliefs. As a result, this minority gathered into groups and communities in order to practice their religious rites, beliefs, and previous traditions. These practices were more linked to witchery and magic than to any other celestial religion. As a result, a movement started in Tunisia, led by the religious men, to persuade the ruler Hammuda Pasha to put an end to their activities and stop their actions for these were in disaccord with the Islamic ways and beliefs. (351)

The merging of the racial and misogynistic discourse in Ahmad Baba's letter is quite significant. Ahmad Baba accuses the Negroes of causing *al-fitna* (chaos, dissension) among Muslims; the same accusation held against women in the Islamic misogynistic tradition:

> When I returned to Tunisia from the Hajj (pilgrimage to Mecca), I found dissensions and infatuations which no one with the tiniest bit of faith in his heart can keep quiet about... Such infatuations do not concern the Jews or the Christians but are the doings of the black KUFFARS (unbelievers) of our country (Tunisia)......The people of Tunis are certain of the polytheism of the Tunisian Negroes, and only few Tunisians have not witnessed their deeds such as slaughtering, prostrating, incense, ablutions of the slaughtered animals and other practices... (351)

Ahmad Baba's attack on the Blacks of Tunisia can be explained by his fear of an emerging matrilineal order. The worshiping of female deities along with the possible alliance between the Negroes and their mistresses constitute a threat to the established patriarchal order:

> Another day someone (a Black slave), wondered why I did not visit "my mother" and I was shown a place that looked like a grave, with some clothes

over it. When I reached the place, I recited parts of the Qur'an, thinking this was the grave of a pious woman. Then a friend asked me: "do you visit an idol?" I said: "no; but the grave of a pious woman." Then he told me the truth about the toys.[2] When I came back from the hajj, a woman (a Black) servant came to me while I was sitting in the shop of a man from Timbuktu. The woman asked me for some money and upon asking her what she would do with that money, she answered that they wanted to play at the 'ajuz's (the old woman's place), who is their idol. I answered her that I would have given her the money if she were going to the mosque.

... Don't you realize O Prince that many of the Moslem women are participating in their atrocities and that their husbands have no power over them? For you know that the men these days are under that authority of their women who rule them...

... The behavior of these Negroes will mark the ruin of this land because they have taken the money of your land unjustly, perfidly, and aggressively. They have taken from these women amounts of money so great that we cannot count it, and this for the purpose of worshipping the jin and lesbianism. They have caused the Moslem women to spend the money of their husbands for the same purpose.

... You should appoint a keeper upon them who know about correct manners and you should force the women away from their Negroes, for women are weak in mind and religion.(353)

Thus, if the alliance between blacks and women is feared, it is because Islamic orthodoxy associates polytheism with the forces of the feminine. In "The Black Merchant," there are two villains who disrupt the established patriarchal order: the black merchant and Settoute. In the initial situation, the wife is secluded. Before leaving the town, the husband buys her a store of food for a year. In "The Magical Grain," both Settoute and the black slave are associated with chaos and the forces that oppose the prevailing culture. "The old sorceress" pushes the male figures to leave the town, thus creating a small matriarchal unit consisting of the mother, the newly born daughter and a female slave. Besides causing the departure of the brothers, Settoute pushes the daughter to challenge the gender roles defined by Islamic Orthodoxy. The girl leaves the house and searches for her brothers in the wilderness of the desert, thus assuming a role traditionally assigned to men. Had the brothers not left, the black slave would never have taken the horse, the clothes, and the white girl's bed. If the black woman is killed at the end, it is because in usurping the identity of her white mistress, she has undermined the hierarchical system underlying Muslim society.

The imagery centered on disease suggests that the black woman's ascendancy to power is a threat to the entire Muslim order. Listening to the white girl's laments, six of the seven camels she is taking care of stop eating when they hear her singing:

> Rise, Rise o rock,Rise, o Rock
>
> Let me see my parents' homeland!
>
> The Negro in the house dwells
>
> And I, a camel-keeper
>
> Weep, O camels, as I weep (15-16)

Only the seventh camel, which is deaf, keeps on eating and filling himself up. The others now look thin and sick to the great worry of the seven brothers. The concordance between the number of the brothers and the camels is not a small detail. Indeed, the number seven is a holy number in the Islamic tradition: God created earth in seven days, people get married in seven days, Muslims fast seven days to atone for their sins, the pious perform the *Hajj* ritual seven times, etc.... Hence, the possible death of the camels signifies not only the ruin of the seven brothers, but also the collapse of the entire Muslim order.

According to Julia Kristeva, "the amoral oscillator," is "he who, slyly and unpredictably, at one time conforms to existing moral principles, and at another secretly flouts them. In a word the one who is abject lacks authenticity, that is, lacks any detectable moral consistency" (John Lechte 160). The association of blacks with the abject is caused by their embracing of two cultural systems: their old African culture and Islamic patriarchy. It is the fear of the border and its dissemination that makes Islamic patriarchy accuse them of witchcraft, polytheism, and even "lesbianism" (Limam 354). Ahmad Baba's letter illustrates quite well this fear of the border:

> The Negroes worship these idols and sacrifice to them, and no one can touch them unless he has done his ablutions... They claim that Kambar has descended from heaven and that she had previously been with Bilal (one of the closed companions of the prophet Md. He was a black man). May he have God's blessings... For example, there is at Dar Janfar, a god called Danuf to whom they sacrifice and whom they paint with blood. Inside the head of each (black) servant, is to be found a jin, to whom they sacrifice and whom they worship... (Limam 352)

Even though most of the blacks in North Africa converted to Islam, they retained their old African religions. This has provided the Arab slaver-holders with an excuse to continue their enslavement.

The fear of Blacks is accompanied by the discourse of miscegenation. In "The Black Merchant," the villain is "a mulatto, probably born out of the union between a white man and a black woman." Under Islamic law, it was both legally and morally correct for a man to have sexual relations with his female slaves. The children born of such a relationship—provided that the father acknowledged paternity—assumed the status of freemen, and had equal standing with other children in the family born by his free wives. The slave mother, having acquired the status of *umm walad* (mother of child), could no longer be sold, and on her master's death became free. However, sexual relations between free women and their slaves were forbidden. Even though Islam does not condemn interracial marriage, Islamic orthodoxy held contemptible the marriage of an Arab woman with a black man. In his letter, Ahmad Baba asks the Ruler of Tunisia to "prevent the marriage between the Negroes and the Moslem women [and to] order the inhabitants not to free a slave before knowing his religion" (Rached Limam 354).

The black woman's ability to change her color in "The Magical Grain" should be examined in view of what Kristeva calls the abject. In *The Powers of Horror*, Kristeva writes:

> It is... not lack of cleanliness or health that causes abjection but what disturbs identity, system, order. What does not respect borders, positions, rules. The in-between, the ambiguous, the composite. (4)

If the black servant is severely punished at the end, it is because in changing her skin color, she has transgressed society's racial and gender frontiers. It is significant that order is restored only when a pious old man intervenes and redraws the boundary of color. To unmask the real black woman, this patriarchal figure advises the seven brothers to unveil the two women: "The only thing a Negro woman cannot change is the texture of her hair. A Negro woman's hair is always kinky, even though her skin has the whiteness of milk" (17). Following the advice of the old man, the seven brothers ask both women to dye their hair with henna. As the black slave refuses to uncover her hair, the seven brothers tear away her veil and reveal her "thorny" hair. It is this transgression of hudud Allah (God's frontiers) which causes her death. In another version of the tale, her punishment is more cruel. The seven brothers tie her hands and feet to four camels. Under the lashes of whips, the animals depart, tearing her to pieces.

Besides the demonization of the feminine and blacks, both tales abide by the Islamic concept of genealogy and kinship. In the Koran, one fulfills half of his or her religious duties by marrying. The absence of kinship signifies the lack of moral principles. As Mernissi puts it:

> As a protective device against zina, marriage is highly recommended to believers of both sexes. A sexually frustrated member of the community is considered dangerous. This is the main reason why Islam is opposed to

> asceticism and requires believers with pious and saintly vocations to acquire pious wives. Abstinence and celibacy are vehemently discouraged." (*Beyond the veil* 59)

Because of his celibacy, the black merchant is demonized. He induces his victims into gambling—a sin according to Islamic law—and causes their ruin. Settoute has no family either; this old woman is either roaming the streets or hobbling in the wilderness. It is significant that in both tales, Settoute lives on the border of culture: she is either in the street ("The Black Merchant's Tale") or near a fountain ("The Magical Grain"). Both this closeness to nature and lack of attachment make her the villain of the North African folktales. In "The Stories of the Seven Dannu sisters,"[3] which deal with the wickedness of old women, each of the sisters believing to do good triggers off a series of catastrophes which make her disowned and repudiated by her own offspring.

However, both tales show resistance towards the same ideology to which they seem to conform. In "The Black Merchant," women put an end to their seclusion and fear of the outside world which Islamic patriarchy defines as a primarily male space. As the tale demonstrates, slave women enjoyed greater liberty than the legitimate spouse: it is the slave, not the wife, who purchases the slaves, the camels, and the goods. This relationship to space is important if we remember women's seclusion and identification with the space they live in; in Arabic the word *dar* (or house) also means woman. As Soumaya Naamane-Guessous remarks, men are reluctant to allude to their wives in the presence of strangers; they would even use phrases like *"al-dar hachak,"* meaning "the house, may God protect you" (*Au dela de toute Pudeur*, 130). The wife's success in rescuing her husband signals a broader and a new definition of womanhood. The wife's ability to restore the entire fortune of her husband undermines the view that women's place is the house.

Throughout "The Magical Grain," water—often a feminine symbol—is associated with border-crossings. The proximity of the fountain of the black women to the fountain of the white women is indicative of the fluidity of identity. The ability to change one's color deconstructs the category of race. It is the white woman's internalization of Islamic patriarchy that makes her remote from the experiences of other women. Settoute's presence at a fountain and use of an acorn to fill her jug suggest a world view that links the feminine to nature.

The white girl's rejection of Settoute and killing of her black slave indicate the supremacy of the racial prerogative over the gender consideration. The images of the ravens and the dove—the hunter/prey—are significant in that they show how women contribute to their own oppression by perpetuating the system of their victimization. This helps explain the sarcastic ending of the tale. The happy ending ironically results in the white woman's seclusion and enslavement:

> The seven brothers returned to their favorite hobby: hunting. The sister cooked and took care of the house. The following spring, mallow plants have grown where the slave woman's ashes are buried. The sister cooks them for her brothers. The seven brothers are instantly transformed into ravens and the girl into a dove. (18)

So far, there has been practically no research on the North African slave narratives. This area is worth investigating not just because these stories are narrated from the oppressor's perspective, but because the history of slavery in the Maghreb is deliberately kept hidden from public knowledge.   Although Blacks constitute an important part of the population of modern Algeria, Morrocco, and the South of Tunisia, the history of slavery is taught neither in high schools nor at the university level; the existence of slavery remains a taboo. If modern Muslim scholars avoid the issue of slavery and prefer to leave it concealed in the mist of time, it is because their acknowledgement that some hadiths were once fabricated to justify slavery, brings into focus contemporary patriarchy's manipulation of the sacred; a weapon often used to sanctify women's oppression. In modern Muslim society, the governing class still holds the sacred text as a weapon to muffle those voices which spring up now and then to advocate social reform.[4] The resemblance between the incident of the Harlots of Hadramaut and the Rushdie's affair—both are accused of apostasy and condemned to the death penalty—points to Islamic patriarchy's entrapment within a past of its own creation. Thus, the dread of revising Islamic history, of acknowledging the construction of hadiths, and of recognizing women's rights betrays the Muslim world's malaise or fear of modernity.

NOTES

1. In Tunisian folklore, the seven sisters are often referred to as the Settoute sisters.
2. Ahmad Baba does not explain what he means by toys. But it is quite probable that he is referring to some magical practices performed by the Blacks of Tunisia
3. These are Tunisian folktales which have not been translated yet.
4. The affair of *The Satanic Verses* exemplifies the use of the sacred as a political weapon. In deconstructing the concept of authority, Rushdie undermines the very basis of the established theocratic states, hence the *fatwa* decree.

BIBLIOGRAPHY

Ahmed, Leila. *Women and Gender in Islam/Historical Roots of a Modern Debate.* New Haven: Yale University Press,1992.

Abdallah, Fadel. "Islam, Slavery, and Racism: The Use of Strategy in the Pursuit of Human Rights." *The American Journal of Islamic Social Science*s 4.1 (1987): 31-50.

Amrouche, Marguerite Taos. "Le Grain Magique." *Le Grain Magique.* Paris: François Maspero, 1971.

Aroui, Abdelaziz. "Tajir al-Akhal." *Hikayat al-Aroui.* Vol I. Tunis: Dar Attunissiya li Nashr, 1989.

Bouhdiba, Abdelwahab. *Sexuality in Islam.* Trans. Alan Sheridan. London: Routlege & Kegan Paul, 1985.

Clissold, Stephen. *The Barbary Slaves*: Totowa: Rowman and Littlefield, 1977.

Guessous Naamane, Soumaya. *Au dela de toute pudeur.* Casablanca: L'Imprimerie Eddar El Beida, 1987.

Gordon, Murray. *Slavery in the Arab World.* New York: New Amsterdam Books, 1989.

Hunwick, J. O. "Black Africans in the Islamic World: An Understudied Dimension of the Black Diaspora." *Tarikh* 5 (1978):20-40.

Laroui, Abdelaziz. "Le marchant noir." *Vieux contes de Tunisie.* Tunis: Maison Tunisienne de l'Edition, 1978.

Lechte, John. *Julia Kristeva.* London: Routledge, 1990.

Lewis, Bernard. *Race and Slavery in the Middle East/A Historical Enquiry.* New York: Oxford University Press, 1990.

Limam, Rached. "Some Documents concerning Slavery in Tunisia at the End of the 18th Century." *Revue d'histoire Maghrebine* 23-24 (1982): 349-357.

Mernissi, Fatima. *Beyond the Veil/Male-Female Dynamics in Modern Muslim Society.* Cambridge: Al Saqi Books, 1975

_______ *The Veil and the Male Elite/A Feminist Interpretation of Women's Rights in Islam.* Trans. Mary Jo Lakeland. New York: Addison-Wesley Publishing Company, 1991.

Norris, H. T. *The Berbers in Arabic Literature.* London: Librairie du Liban, 1982.

Propp, Vladimir. "Morphology of the Folktale." *International Journal of American Linguistics* 24.4 (Oct 1958): 1-134

_______ *Theory and History of Folklore.* Trans. Ariadna Y. Martin and Richard P. Martin. Manchester: Manchester University Press, 1984

Savage, Elizabeth, ed. *The Human Commodity: Perspectives on the Trans-Saharan Slave Trade*. London: Frank Cass & Co. Ltd, 1992.

Willis, John Ralph. *Slaves and Slavery in Muslim Africa*. Vol 1. London: Frank Cass, 1985.

CONTRIBUTORS

S. Ekema Agbaw teaches African American and Non-Western literatures at Bloomsburg University of Pennsylvania. Before getting to Bloomsburg, he had taught at University of Connecticut, Dickinson College and the University of Yaounde, Cameroon. His research interests include African interpretations of English and American literatures, post-modern narratives of slavery, and contemporary African fiction and film.. He co-edits a newsletter, *Making Connections,* for teachers of culturally diverse literatures.

Jean-Pierre Bekolo is in the avant-garde of current African filmmaking, having directed *Quartier Mozart* and *Aristotle's Plot*.

Lamia Ben Youssef is currently a doctoral student in the English Department at Michigan State University. She has taught American and British literature for three years at the Faculté des Lettres et des Sciences Humaines et Sociales (Tunis). In May 1995, she received a Fulbright Scholarship to pursue a Ph.D. at Michigan State University.

Assia Djebar is one of the foremost novelists and filmmakers from the Maghreb. Her novels and collections of short stories include *La Soif, Les Enfants du nouveau monde, Les Alouettes naïves, Femmes d'Alger dans leur appartement, L'Amour, la fantasia, Ombre Sultane, Vaste est la prison, Loin de Médine, Oran, langue morte*, and *Le Blanc de l'Algérie*. She has also published *Chronique d'un été algérien*. Her films include *La Nouba des femmes du mont Chenoua* and *La Zerda et les chants de l'oubli*.

Carmela Garritano is a doctoral candidate in the Department of English at Michigan State University. She is writing a dissertation on the construction of gendered and racialized identities in West African video and film.

Jarrod Hayes is an Assistant Professor of French and Francophone Studies at the University of Michigan, Ann Arbor. His articles include "Proust in the Tearoom," *PMLA* (1995), "Approches de l'homosexualité et de l'homoérotisme chez Boudjedra, Mammeri et Sebbar," *Présence Francophone* (1993), and "Rachid O. and the Return of the Homopast: The

Autobiographical as Allegory in Childhood Narratives by Maghrebian Men," forthcoming in *Sites*.

Linda Lizut Helstern is an engineering administrator and adjunct instructor of English at Southern Illinois University at Carbondale. Her articles on contemporary novelists Gerald Vizenor and Louis Owens have appeared in *Studies in American Indian Literatures*.

Gaston Kaboré is one of the foremost African filmmakers, having made *Wend Kuuni*, winner of the Etalon de Yennenga (Stallion of Yennenga) prize in 1983, *Rabi*, and *Zan Boko*. In 1997 he won his second Etalon de Yennenga (Stallion of Yennenga) prize for his film *Budd Yam*, awarded during the 15th edition of FESPACO.

Touria Khannous is currently a Ph.D. student in English at Brown University. She has had a Fulbright scholarship for Sidi Mohammed Ben Abdellah University in Fes, Morocco, and is currently researching topics in postcolonial theory, film criticism, and African women's literature and film.

Lydie Moudileno is an Assistant Professor of French in the Department of Romance Languages at the University of Pennsylvania. She is the author of *L'Ecrivain antillais au miroir de sa littérature*, and of several articles on Caribbean and African literature.

Ngozi Onwurah is a Nigerian-born black British filmmaker and has made over twenty films. Her films include, *The Body Beautiful*, *Poppy*, *Monday's Girls*, *And Still I Rise*, *Who Stole the Show*, *Flight of the Swan*, *White Men Are Cracking Up*, *Behind the Mask*, *I Bring You Frankincense*, *"Welcome II the Terrordome*, and *Coffee Colored Children*. She has also written and directed several film projects for the BBC TV.

Stephen Zacks is a master's degree student in the Committee on Liberal Studies of the Graduate Faculty of Political and Social Science at the New School for Social Research in New York City. His other articles include "The Theoretical Construction of African Cinema" in *Research in African Literatures* (Volume 26, Number 3), and "A Problematic Sign of African Difference" in *Matatu: Journal for African Culture and Society* (Number 19).

EDITORS

Maureen N. Eke is an Assistant Professor of English at Central Michigan University, Mt. Pleasant, where she teaches courses in African, African American, and World Literatures, as well as literature and film. Some of her publications include, "Revisioning African Drama to Include the Female Voice: Fatima Dike, a Revolutionary Dramatist" in *Doing Feminism: Teaching and Research in the Academy*. Michigan State University Press, 1997. Her articles have appeared in *Callaloo*, *Visual Anthropology*, and the *South African Theatre Journal*. Her research interests include Black women's writing, drama, African cinema, as well as post-colonial literatures and theory.

Kenneth W. Harrow is a professor of English at Michigan State University. He has published *Thresholds of Change in African Literature*, and has edited *Faces of Islam in African Literature*, *The Marabout and the Muse*, *African Cinema: Postcolonial and Feminist Readings*, a special issue of *RAL* on African cinema, and *Women with Open Eyes*, a special issue of *Matatu* on women and African cinema. He is completing a study of feminism and African women's literature, *The Other (Side of the) Mirror*.

Emmanuel Yewah teaches French and comparative literature at Albion College (Michigan). His publications have appeared in *Research in African Literatures*, *African Literature Today*, *Theatre Research International*, *Callaloo*, *The French Review*. His teaching and research focus on literature and politics, cultural studies, African detective fiction,the Critical Legal Studies Movement, and the cross-examination of law and literature.

INDEX